CONTRIBUTIONS OF NGOs FOR SOCIAL DEVELOPMENT ANDHRA PRADESH

CONTRIBUTIONS OF NGOs FOR SOCIAL DEVELOPMENT ANDHRA PRADESH
(Vizianagaram)

Karanam Viswa Bhushan

KALPAZ

ISBN : 978-93-5128-193-1
Price : ₹ 850

First Published, 2016

Published by

Kalpaz Publications
C-30, Satyawati Nagar,
Delhi-110052
Ph. : 9212142040
E-mail: kalpaz@hotmail.com

Printed at : G. Print Process, Delhi

Cataloging in Publication Data—DK
Courtesy: D.K. Agencies (P) Ltd. <docinfo@dkagencies.com>

Bhushan, Karanam Viswa, author.
A study on the contributions of non-governmental organisations (NGOs) : for social development in the Vizianagaram District, Andhra Pradesh, India / Karanam Viswa Bhushan.
pages cm
Includes bibliographical references.
ISBN 9789351281931

1. Non-governmental organizations—India—Vizianagaram (District)—History. 2. Social change—India—Vizianagaram (District)—History. I. Title.
JZ4841.B48 2016 DDC 361.77095485 23

Dedicated

to

My Parents

Contents

Acknowledgements

I would like to express my sincere gratitude to Dr. T. Sobha Sri, Associate Professor, Department of Social Work, Andhra University, Visakhapatanam, Andhra Pradesh, for her constant guidance, valuable suggestions and encouragement throughout my research study.

I am thankful to my brother Dr. K. Pushpanadham, Associate Professor, Department of Educational Administration, The M. S. University of Baroda, Vadodara, Gujarat for his expertise and subtle suggestions for the completion of the study.

I am extremely thankful to Professor K.Visweswara Rao, Department of Social Work, Andhra University, for his constant encouragement and support.

I am immensely grateful to Dr. A.B.S.V. Ranga Rao, Associate Professor, Department of Social Work, Andhra University for his co-operation and guidance.

I am extremely grateful to Dr. K. Hanumatha Rao, Director, M. R. Post-Graduate College, Vizianagaram for his word of encouragement and support.

I am immensely thankful to Y.Ravi kumar (Glod Medal Awardee) Associate professor and former Head of the Department of philosophy M.R.College, Vizianagaram for his benevolent help.

I am highly thankful to my twin brother Rev. Fr. K. Dhaman Kumar who prayed for me and extended unstinted support from the beginning of this endeavour.

I am thankful to my colleagues Sri. R. Srinivasu, Sri. K. Srinivasu and D.Vanaja who propelled me towards my goal with their suggestions and assistance.

I am greatly indebted to all the functionaries and beneficiaries of NGOs for their cooperation and willingness to respond to the study.

It is indeed my privilege to extend my heartfelt gratitude to my parents, brothers and sisters for their constant encouragement and support.

Last but not least I shall remain ever grateful to all those who supported me at various levels in bringing the research study into thesis for submission.

I sincerely extend my spiritual thanks to the God Almighty.

Karanam Viswa Bhushan

Chapter - I

Overview of Non-Governmental Organisations

1

Overview of Non-Governmental Organisations

1.1 Introduction

"The future is not of ease or resting, but of incessant striving so that we may fulfill the pledge we have so often taken and the one we shall take today. The service of India means the service of the millions who suffer. It means the ending of poverty and ignorance and disease and inequality of opportunity. The ambition of the greatest men of our generation has been to wipe every fear from every eye. That may be beyond us. But as long as there are tears and suffering, so long our work may not be over." (Pandit Jawaharlal Nehru - 1947)

The non-governmental organizations (NGOs) have gained increased attention among scholars and practitioners of development. They have become increasingly important agents of the development process in the countries, in all of their main areas of work such as humanitarian relief, long-term development, policy formation and political advocacy (Attack 1999). On the other hand, there is a current view that NGOs constitute a viable alternative to government as channels of development assistance, particularly in developing countries. Some of the NGO's functions and advantages, according to Streeten (1997) are: (1) they are good at reaching and mobilizing the poor and remote communities; (2) they help empower poor people to gain control of their lives, and they work with and strengthen local institutions; (3) they carry out projects at lower costs and more efficiently than the government agencies and (4) they promote sustainable development.

In the process of realizing the vision of democratic, egalitarian, welfare and Development oriented glorious Indian Society; the contributions have come from all disciplines, fields and sectors. Social work and voluntary organizations or voluntarism and Voluntary action, now popularly known as NGOs are not the exceptions. Voluntary Organizations promoting service to humanity as in the past, their roots in religion became part of system charity under feudal economy. They have assumed an active role as contributors of the developing society under capitalistic and socialistic system. Social work today in India is not merely a leisure time activity but also has assumed the greater role in helping people to help themselves by providing professional services with definite knowledge, techniques, attitude, values and skills which are acquired by social workers to help individual, groups and communities with the objective of treatment, prevention, promotion, rehabilitation, welfare, development and empowerment.

Social work is basically an interventionist and practice oriented profession. Pincus and Minahan (1973) has given its major aim as follows : " Social work is concerned with the interactions between people and their social environment which effect the ability of people to accomplish their life tasks, alleviate distress, and realize their aspirations and values. The purpose of social work therefore is to (i) enhance the problem solving and coping capacities of people, (ii) link people with systems that provide them with resources, services and opportunities, (iii) prómote the effective and humane operation of these systems, and (iv) contribute to the development and improvement of social policy.

According to National Association of Social Workers (1973), Social Work is the professional activity of helping individuals, groups or communities enhance or restore their capacity for social functioning and creating societal conditions favorable to this goal.

Social Work practice consists of the professional application of social work values, principles and techniques to one or more of the following ends: (i) helping people obtain tangible services, (ii) counseling and psychotherapy with individuals, families & groups, (iii) helping communities or groups provide social and health services and (iv) participating in relevant legislative processes. The significance of social work and NGOs in the development processes is being increasingly realized by the world including India. Both of them have assumed the status of in-built institutions or organizations in the society.

1.2 Meaning of Non-governmental Organizations (NGOs)

The acronym NGO is not very helpful in describing the organizations it defines, in that it tells us what the organizations are not, rather than what they are. The term 'NGO' dates from 1950, when the United Nations coined the expression (Vakil, 1997, 2068). Presumably the UN, which dealt primarily with governments and wanted to consult private, non-profit organizations that were independent of governments, found it convenient to refer to them simply as NGOs to distinguish them from governments. Today the United Nations (2003) describe an NGO as follows: any non-profit, voluntary citizens' group which is organized on a local, national or international level. Task-oriented and driven by people with a common interest, NGOs perform a variety of services and humanitarian functions, bring citizens' concerns to Governments, monitor policies and encourage political participation at the community level. They provide analysis and expertise, serve as early warning mechanisms and help monitor and implement international agreements. Some are organized around specific issues, such as human rights, the environment or health. In the remainder of this article, we focus on social purpose NGOs (referring to them simply as 'NGOs') and define them as follows: NGOs are private, not-for-profit organizations that aim to serve particular societal interests by focusing advocacy and/ or operational efforts on social, political and economic goals, including equity, education, health, environmental protection and human rights. Having defined NGOs as the organizational manifestations of civil society interests, we now discuss the role and functions of

NGOs relative to their public- and private-sector counterparts (governments and firms, respectively) in value creation and governance globally.

"Non-Governmental Organization" is a term that encompasses a wide range of similar and dissimilar organizations. NGOs are private and pursue a variety of activities that enhance the general welfare of the communities they serve. They may be secular or religious, and often work in tandem with national and local governments, regional groupings and/or international bodies. One of their major strengths, however, lies in their ability to maintain institutional autonomy and political neutrality. These two factors are more important for some NGO's than others, and not always possible to attain. Government/NGO collaboration is both a common and desirable feature in many international development programs organized under foreign aid initiatives or by foreign aid donors. Maintaining institutional autonomy and political neutrality in some of these cases is a tremendous challenge. Failure to maintain autonomy and neutrality may severely jeopardize goal achievement, threaten the stability of an already unstable situation, and compromise the NGOs legitimacy to work in given countries.

Unfortunately, if governments or warring factions implicitly or explicitly expect and insist upon political allegiance, NGOs face the dilemma of either violating their position on neutrality or failing to provide needed services to citizens who are victims of a conflict they did not generate and are powerless to control. Examples of this in the world today are abundant. Indeed, some international NGOs administering emergency assistance in trouble-torn countries have been asked to leave for political reasons. Others have left because the safety of their personnel could not be guaranteed, or because their neutrality or sovereignty was threatened, thus compromising their stated mission. Non-secular NGOs may have a more difficult time maintaining political neutrality in a country torn by ethnic and/ or religious strife.

Characteristics that differentiate the range of organizations operating under the NGO banner include: size, organizational structure, nature of national and international affiliation, mission, operational program areas, geographic location, administrative efficiency, accountability, financial resources and funding sources, level of coordination with government and other NGOs, and membership criteria. Strategies used ranging from grass roots/local community organization, education, leadership development, policy development and implementation, empowerment through local and national coalition building to human rights and social justice.

Target populations include specific categories of the poor and disenfranchised; age and gender-specific groups; selected occupational groups (e.g. farmers and fishermen); and persons adversely affected by disease, natural and man-made disasters, ethnic strife and forced migration. Many NGOs work together as a team locally and nationally, especially in programs aimed at poverty alleviation, sustainable development, and disaster relief. They may be a part of a larger effort coordinated by an international body such as the United Nations and its specialized agencies (UNICEF, WHO, UNHCR) or by multinational organizations such as the International Committee of the Red Cross, Oxfam, Save the Children Federation, and Medicines sans Frontiers. Large NGOs have offices in many countries, employ paid staff, and do organized fund-raising. They often cut across populations and are multi-task oriented if their mission includes relief and humanitarian aid, social development, advocacy, education, and empowerment, health care and general welfare promotion. NGOs specializing in technological innovation are invaluable team members for many social development projects. Small NGOs may depend entirely on voluntary efforts for program implementation and membership contributions for funding, which may limit their impact.

The major advantages of NGOs include their flexibility, ability to innovate, grass-roots orientation, humanitarian vs. commercial goal orientation, non-profit status, dedication and commitment, and recruitment philosophy. Many are made up of volunteers so deeply committed to the NGOs mission that they are willing to undergo considerable hardships and no monetary compensation in order to carry out that mission. In addition to supporting innovation, NGOs may serve as pilots for larger anticipated projects, help to motivate and involve community based organizations whose constituents may be the primary beneficiaries of a larger project, serve as advocates are in a unique position to share communication both horizontally and vertically. A close look at the implementation strategy of any given country's development plan will reveal the nature and extent of NGO activity in relation to its current circumstances. Relief for families and children affected by the AIDS pandemic, local social development, environmental protection, gender equality, the protection of children's rights and freedoms, and promoting the positive and fighting against the ill effects of economic globalization, feature prominently in the list of NGO activities throughout the world today.

Drawbacks in partnering or working with local, national, and international NGOs, to some extent, are the mirror image of the advantages cited above. In addition, disadvantages cited in the literature concerned with sustainable social development, and as reported from the field, include: over-zealousness, restricted local participation, inadequate feasibility studies, conflicts or misunderstanding with the host partner (usually resulting from a poorly negotiated contract and lack of safeguards), inflexibility in recruitment and procedures, lack of adequate funding to complete or sustain projects, inadequately trained personnel, turf issues, lack of transparency, inadequate or non-existent evaluation component and research expertise, inability to replicate results, and cultural insensitivity. Many NGOs operating on a restricted budget fail to include a feasibility and evaluation component. This has been shown repeatedly to be a serious and costly omission.

With regard to cultural insensitivity, national (if the country is multi-ethnic) and international NGOs have a responsibility to ensure that the services provided are suitable to the population being served. While this appears to be obvious, some projects involving NGOs operate on the "one size fits all" model. Cultural sensitivity and cultural relevance are particularly important when matters of health and welfare are concerned. An ethnic group's response to illness, wellness, tragedy, natural disaster, and up-rootedness is embedded in its cultural and religious beliefs and practices. For example, if mass relocation of a population is necessary to meet an important development goal, cooperation may depend upon how local deities are accommodated in the relocation. Many international NGO personnel arriving on the scene to dispense humanitarian aid were surprised at the lack of relief camps at the border. The NGO supplies included equipment generally found to be essential in such camps. Relying on the existence of a strong extended family system characteristic of this country, the government put in place a plan for transporting incoming nationals immediately to their hometown or location of ethnic origin. This avoided the hardship and squalor usually associated with emergency squatter arrangements, and placed the initial responsibility for resettlement on the returnees' families and community. The NGOs then had to re-evaluate the role they needed to play in this cultural context.

Efforts to manage the AIDS crisis in many countries hit by this pandemic would not be successful without the dedication of local, national, and international NGOs. Local NGOs have played a vital role in tailoring government and private response to the cultural practices of local populations. The extent to which information and efforts to change behaviour are geared to the cultural beliefs of the local population can make or break a development, relief or prevention program. Because many development programs–especially health–focus on KAB (knowledge, attitude and behavior), it is critical at the design stage to understand the psychological components of attitude development and change within a given cultural context. International NGO's with national and local counterparts have the advantage of input and feedback from their local affiliates in designing culturally appropriate programs. This input should not be overlooked or minimized.

Countries have different criteria for official recognition of NGOs. It must be noted that not all NGOs listed on websites in various countries meet even the country's definition of an NGO, and would not meet either formal or informal international criteria. Many countries require NGOs to register - partially for monitoring their non-profit status. This registration procedure also helps potential donors and relief agencies to identify suitable NGO partners.

Criteria, processes and procedures that are likely to maximize success and sustainability of projects, as identified by individual NGOs, partnering agencies or organizations and financial institutions (Global Development Research Center, 2003; World Bank, 1995) includes:

1. Selecting the appropriate NGO through careful identification and review of relevant criteria, outlining a selection process based on project specific needs, assessing the NGO's organizational capacity based on its track record and not its stated goal, and maximizing transparency in the selection process;
2. Seeking NGO input during all phases of the project including project and site identification, feasibility study, design, implementation and evaluation;
3. Awareness of time issues, including need for extra start-up time; preparation for time lags and the risks they pose to the participatory process; unavoidable timeframe changes due to acts of nature, delivery delays, technical mishaps and failures (too often underestimated); and awareness of the capacity of all participants to meet stated deadlines;
4. Building in community input in the early stages, establishing an effective feedback process, identifying important levels and modes of communication that are culturally relative and sensitive, establishing a periodic review process, and establishing flexibility in adopting structures, procedures, activities (and possibly goals) in the light of changing or unforeseen local conditions;
5. Clarifying funding arrangements by establishment of agreement on mutually acceptable fees, overhead costs, re-imbursements, cost sharing, advance payments, donation of project equipment, and nature of in-kind contributions.
6. In some countries, proposed international collaborative projects, especially those that include a research component

and/or involvement of local populations, need approval from the national body responsible for monitoring research or projects in the country. This is designed to protect the citizenry from obtrusive intrusion of their privacy, to ensure that the research goals fit the country's social development plan and are in the best interest of the country, to protect the data base, to validate the competency of the research team, and to ensure that results are shared with the appropriate local personnel. This oversight function is often performed through a university, by a government or quasi-government sociological/economic/demographic institute involved in local social development or by an organization designated by the government.

A clear contract setting out terms of agreement, taking into account the above-listed criteria, processes and procedures and other relevant issues, is essential. Government/NGO collaboration may not be appropriate in all situations. In cases where formal contracts are problematic, a Memorandum of Understanding or alternative forms of contract may be substituted. Attention to NGO capacity building, training of relevant staff and involvement of relevant local, national and international NGOs require consideration. An NGO liaison person may be valuable asset.

Some countries have hundreds of NGOs with or without national and international affiliation. Many international NGOs are in consultative status with UNICEF and belong to the NGO Committee on UNICEF. The author highlights below the UNICEF/NGO partnership because of its success, relevance to a vulnerable population worldwide, adherence to criteria and procedures outlined above for partnership development, and its documentation in the literature.

The United Nations recognizes the vital role that civil society organizations play in partnership with governments, UN agencies, and others. A recent example of this type of partnership was reflected in the General Assembly Special Session for Children held at United Nations headquarters in 2002. More than 1700 NGO representatives from 88 different countries attended the Special Session. The NGO Steering Group and the NGO Committee on UNICEF commended the work of NGOs in the life saving achievements for children since their coming into force of the Convention on the Rights of the Child (UNCRC). Holding governments accountable for the existence of conditions inimical to the welfare of children, seeing that children have a "first call" on distribution of national resources, protecting children from HIV/AIDS, sexual exploitation, war and other violence, attaining equality for the girl child and women, monitoring National Plans of Action and the implementation of the Outcome Document in relation to the UNCRC, and promotion of the Global Partnership for Children and Adolescents are recognized as vital NGO activities (NGO Committee on UNICEF, 2000, 2002). United Nations reports resulting from world summits, special sessions and conferences on social development, women, the environment, human settlements, population, trade, the elderly, armed conflict and peace-keeping operations, and their follow-up meetings also highlight the importance of the role of NGOs, including many that are not in partnership with the United Nations. There is a global NGO community network website for non-governmental organizations associated with the United Nations. It provides up-to-date information on United Nations Department of Public Information briefings, United Nations meetings and conferences, and news related to issues before the General Assembly.

For persons interested in the formal study of NGO management and development, there are short and long-term term courses given within and outside university settings around the world. Some courses target NGO staff members; others target NGO government partners. Courses are aimed at both the experienced and the novice. Prominent themes include program/project and policy development, human resource development, fundraising and financial management, lobbying, setting action agendas, conflict resolution, data collection and management, monitoring and evaluation. Some programs include creative educational and training collaborations across national boundaries. Information is available on NGO web sites.

It has been established that NGOs can make and have made invaluable contributions to the social and economic development process of various countries. The successes and challenges of NGO partnerships have been demonstrated and documented in country-specific and international social/economic development reports and journals related to social development. Because of this documentation, individuals, agencies, governments, and financial institutions wishing to work with NGOs now have clearer guidelines for achieving success and avoiding the mistakes of the past. Continued efforts by Foreign Aid Ratings to develop international criteria for rating and listing NGOs should make national and local partnering more efficient and effective.

The present century has witnessed a phenomenal change in all walks of life around the globe. However, the patterns of structural inequalities often exclude people, such as those in rural areas, women, youth, people with disabilities, and other historically disadvantaged social groups. These patterns are more clear and visible in the developing countries. India as an emerging giant is also undergoing such challenges and trying to uplift the social standards by minimizing the inequalities through education, employment, health and industrialization. The government of India has put in place public policies and programs to redress these inequities. Nonetheless, many of these social groups have been unable to tap into the prosperity that others enjoy, often because they are unable to hold those in power accountable. Lack of inclusion and accountability can cause disruptions that discourage investment, reduce growth and threaten the cohesiveness of societies.

UN Millennium Development Goals (MDGs) have advocated for the adoption comprehensive and inclusive strategies that empower poor and marginalized people to take advantage of burgeoning global opportunities. Economic growth is essential for the world to meet the MDGs. Only with the additional resources, the growth generates and countries can invest in better services for poor women and men. However, this growth needs to be pro-poor and sustainable. For growth to benefit poor people, development agencies need to invest in human and physical assets. In addition, development agencies need to help transform the broad set of institutions that determine the quality of growth, service delivery and human development. The world won't meet the MDGs without complementary economic and social development efforts.

1.3 Historical Development of NGOs in india

NGOs in India are the product of social, ethical, economic, political, democratic, cultural and religious values and considerations. Its recorded history is around 150 years old. Today number of voluntary organizations working in different fields of social services, social welfare, social development, empowerment etc. are on increase. NGOs emerged in India soon after Independence when Mahatma Gandhi made a plea for dissolving the Indian National Congress (the political Party which came into power upon Independence), and transforming it into a LokSevakSangh (Public Service Organization). This plea was, however, rejected; nevertheless, it did not halt the formation of non-governmental organizations in India. Many followers of Mahatma Gandhi established voluntary agencies to work closely with the governmental programs on social and economic issues. These agencies organized handicrafts and village industries, rural development programs, credit cooperatives, educational institutions, etc. Many voluntary organizations like all India spinners association (1925), All India Villages' Industries Association (1934) were active in this era.

The second stage of growth of NGOs in India was around 1960 when many individuals noticed that the governmental programs seemed to be inadequate to deal with the deprived sections of India.

These groups formed organizations that worked on behalf of the poor, the landless, the tribal, the bonded labourers, and many other social groups that were being discriminated against by the policies of the state and social structure. These grass root organizations work at the micro-level and work with limited resources and lack of coordination. Since independence in 1947 until around 1980, there was little effort on the part of the Indian Government to define the role of a voluntary agency or to recognize its importance. During the Janata regime, infact, there was a strong emphasis on voluntary agencies and the Fifth Draft Plan supported the development of NGOs and pledged state support to them. In fact there was even a body of opinion that the state should withdraw from development and entrust it to voluntary agencies. In 1980, however, with the Sixth Five Year Plan (1980-1985), the government identified new areas in which NGOs as new actors could participate in development. These areas included : (i) Optimal utilization and development of renewable source of energy, including forestry through the formation of renewable energy association at the block level, (ii) Family Welfare, health and nutrition, education and relevant community programs in the field, (iii) Programes like Health for all, (iv) Water management and soil conservation, (v) Social welfare programs for weaker sections, (vi) implementation of minimum needs program, (vii) Disaster preparedness and management (i.e. for floods, cyclones, etc.), (viii) Promotion of ecology and tribal development and (ix) Environmental protection and education. This plan, nevertheless, was to become the first of a series.

Under the Seventh Five Year Plan (1985-1990), the Indian government envisioned a more active role for voluntary organizations to aid in making communities as self-reliant as possible. These groups were expected to show how village and indigenous resources could be used and how human resources, rural skills and local knowledge, grossly underutilized at present, could be used for their own development. NGOs because of their situation and interaction with local people can be very effective in bringing change since they are able to address issues that governments are often not able to comprehend.

In the Eight Five Year Plan the importance of NGOs is further enhanced, paying particular attention to the role of these agencies as participants in rural appraisal for drawing up development plans at a very low cost and involving the rural community. The plan document states, "A nation-wide network of NGOs will be created. In order to facilitate the working of this network, three schemes relating to the creation, replication, multiplication and consultancy development have been worked out by the Planning Commission." The Nineth Five Year Plan admitted that Panchayati Raj Institution, Cooperative Societies, Self-Help Groups and VOs could play a paramount role in decentralized democracy and participatory development.

In the context of the Tenth Five Year Plan 2002-2007, it became an imperative to examine the prospective role of the VOs. The voluntary sector has witnessed a perceptible change in the thinking of the government when it, in March, 2000, declared the Planning Commission as a 'Nodal Agency' for the GO-VOs interface. This was perhaps due to the ever-increasing role of the VOs and considerable influence of the foreign donor agencies.

This agency acts as a think-tank on VOs and so far, has been performing two major tasks. Viz., creating a database on VOs by displaying information about 13,000 VOs who had received grants from different ministries/departments and 1,000 other good/valid VOs rated by various bilateral, multilateral, intermediary and governmental agencies. The majority of members on the national advisory council are drawn from the non-governmental sector. Aruna Roy heads the Rajasthan-based MazdoorKisan Shakti Sangathan, which has fought an arduous battle for the right to information, Jayaprakash Narayan runs the Hyderabad based Loksatta, well-known for compiling data on the criminalization of politics, MadhavChavan is the brain behind primary education programmes through his voluntary agency, 'Pratham', MirajChatterjee is co-ordinatro social security for SEWA, that outstanding trade union of self-employed women, (SagarikaGhose : The Indian Express, 05/07/2004).

A careful examination of the plan document reveals that VOs during plan period i.e. 2002-2007 are expected to play different role models by executing planners' missions. These are discussed as under the head (i) Social Mobilization, (ii) Strengthening SHGs Capacities, (iii) Imparting Training for Entrepreneurial Abilities, (vi) Sharing Managerial Experiences with Development Bureaucracy and (v) Independent Monitoring and Evaluation. The VOs as outside third parties should be assigned monitoring and evaluation of the rural development programmes, VOs should devise ways and means to improve the performance. They should, at least, pay sincere attention towards some developments happening in the VO field).

Today, India has a vigorous NGO sector, although there has been no complete census of NGOs, it is estimated that about 25,000 to 30,000 are active in India. In fact, as of December 31st, 1989, there were 12,313 NGOs registered with the Ministry of Home Affairs, Government of India under the Foreign Contribution (Regulation) Act (FCRA) 1976. Furthermore, 726 NGOs are unregistered but under the prior permission category. One problem with NGOs in India, as with NGOs anywhere else in the world, has been the increasing dependency on governmental funds or donations from external (foreign) donors like the World Bank. This dependent relationship has resulted in a lack of flexibility on the part of NGOs to pick their missions and objectives since many are expected to perform certain tasks in return for funding. But, further still, it has also created structures that have become more bureaucratic in nature and, hence, less effective in development. NGOs working for rural development in India has also become a significant area of attention. Their number and contribution have become visible and demonstrative. Estimates of the number of NGOs active in rural development in India range from fewer than 10,000 to several hundreds depending on the type of classification used.

A realistic estimate of the number of NGOs actively engaged in rural development in India would be in the 15-20,000 range, including local and regional branches of national organizations which operate as NGOs in their own right. Wide variations in the densities of NGOs exist among states.

The most common type of NGOs in India is the small agency working in a cluster of villages in a particular locality. NGOs especially the larger and more established organizations formed the Voluntary Action Network India (VANI) in April, 1988 as a common platform for NGOs. Nearly 20,000 organizations are registered with the Ministry of Home Affairs for foreign funding.. These numbers are on increase and are going to stay and will continue to work in India on political, economical or social issues, the task before them is how they will manage to produce change will keeping track for governmental documentation, planning commission, central social welfare board, Indian Council Social Welfare etc.

1.4 Non-Governmental Organisations: Alternative Catalyst Of Development

Since the end of the Second World War the developing countries have experienced a period of enormous political and economic change. But countries in the third world which succeeded with industrialization and which also achieved a remarkable economic rate of growth, failed to provide distributive justice to the vast majority of population specially rural poor." Most of the developing countries have plagued with problems of poverty, malnutrition, illiteracy and high mortality despite all the developmental programmes and projects which were implemented and directed towards improving the situation of the rural poor in the last few decades. According to a recent World Development Report, 46.4 per cent- nearly half the world's poor in 1985, lived in South Asia which had roughly 30 per cent of the world's population. Sub-saharan Africa with 16 per cent of the poor and 11 per cent population was another region having a highly disproportionate share of Global poverty. On the other hand East Asia, having 40 per cent of population had only 25 per cent of the poor and rest of the world with 19 per cent of population had 12 per cent of the poor.

Thus, the development experiences of the 1970s and 80s have raised more and more critical questions concerning a growing awareness of limits of the existing development models about the dilemma of the widening gap between the very few rich and the vast majority of the poor in the developing countries." This has given momentum to search for more adequate and appropriate strategies for improving the living conditions of the poor population and started a good deal of discussion about the systematic alternative development strategies such as the integrated development approach ; the basic needs approach, community participation', 'Self help' and 'self-reliance' concepts. It was observed by quite a number of development planners in national and international perspectives that there was a need for new and innovative approaches for a more equal and just development according to the real needs and wishes of the poor population on the basis of the local needs and demands not only for the successful implementation of the proposed development projects but also for their lasting effects. In the course of these analytical discussions, it was felt that modernization concepts, large-scale development programmes where a 'trickle-down' effect was hoped for but rarely achieved and 'top down' planning strategies should be superseded by more poverty oriented, participatory development concept, small scale programmes, and by 'bottom-up' planning procedures.

These alternative concepts, approaches and strategies constitute basic elements of the development of a number of NGOs throughout the world which are giving attention to the definition and projection of a people-centered development vision that embraces the transformation agendas. This vision looks to justice, sustainability and inductiveness as the defining principle of authentic development. It views development as a people's movement more than as a foreign funded government projects. It looks to the government to enable the people to develop themselves. It seeks a synthesis of the change objectives of the environmental, human rights, consumer protection, women's and peace movements. It seeks a new human consciousness in which the more nurturing, enabling and conserving dimensions of female consciousness gain ascendance over the more aggressive, exploitation and competitive dimensions of male consciousness that have so long dominated the social and economic life of human societies. Thus, various resolutions of UN bodies have identified mass sharing of benefits of development, mass contribution to development and mass involvement in the decision making process of development as the three basic ingredients of popular participation.

In this sense, it can be added that economic growth is not an end in itself. It is a means for achieving a set of developmental objectives that are multi-dimensional. If economic growth is to serve the interest of the people, it must address itself to their problems. Hence, economic growth must be able to mount an all-out attach on some of the Worst features of mass poverty and its cases. If this means an increase in employment at the village level the structure of economic growth must fulfill this social goal. Indeed, the objective of people's participation is changing the relationship between human beings within a social and institutional framework in such a way that the objective reality as it reveals itself before the people is no longer a constant, but a variable capable of being consciously transformed for the benefit of all. The process of this transformation, on the other hand, must progressively increase the confidence of the masses in themselves and the institutional complex to solve their problems, with an increasing awareness of the directive of change.

Ultimately, people's participation aims at nothing less than the transformation of man himself form a passive spectator to an active participant, who is capable of consciously defining his relationship with both nature and society in a dynamic frame of references. Thus the success of this principle will not only prove beneficial economically, but above all, it will install in the members a sense of self confidence on their ability to work together for active benefit based on their own resources and efforts. When this is lacking, multi-polar institutional strategy fails to provide the dynamism for economic growth and social change that benefit the masses.

The concern for people's participation does not have a long history. It reflects partly the failure of the "trickle down" model (TDM) of economic development advocated after the end of the Second World War. There is very little evidence of anything trickling down to the common masses. The failure of the trickle down model has caused concern and has set many people thinking about the very meaning of development, the new concern has been reinforced by a few evolving trends. Thus, the search for a viable alternative strategy has become a matter of urgent necessity. What makes the situation different from the past is not the mere existence of mass poverty, but the conscious realization of this fact among an increasing number of people and the knowledge that it should and could be changed. Indeed, mass participation in the implementation of decisions can be effective only when there has been mass participation in the decision making as well.

Hence, mass participation in implementation should be viewed as a system of interlocking relationships between the villagers, the village level institution that mobilized this participation and strengthen the level of institution further up to the national level. In brief it is a model seeking to release what is called the social energy of the people towards attaining the self-defined goals of development. The model ratifies the principle of planning with the people. It complements the macro-planning efforts with micro planning achievements. (It is based on the philosophy of gradual enablement, enlightenment and enfranchisement of the people and is propelled by the social psychology of organized motivation). This model incorporates several of the principles of the Poverty Alleviation Strategies. The basic philosophy behind this model agrees well with the definition of development given by Brown and Korten (1989). They State:

We believe that development is most usefully and accurately defined as: "A process by which the members of a society increase their personal and institutional capacities to mobilize and manage resource to produce sustainable and justly distributed improvements in their quality of life consistent with their own aspirations".

The spirit of the above definition goes to give development a human face. It acknowledges that only the people themselves can define what they consider to be improvements in the quality of their lives. At present, the governments in the developing countries are already overburdened with their involvement in routine works which detract their vision, from national development activities, particularly at the micro level. This reality necessitates that people should participate in minimizing the magnitude of their problems on their own or with the assistance of the government or non-governmental agencies. It is this context that creates enough of scope for non-governmental organization (NGOs) to step into the scene for what a World Bank document (1991) describes as "galvanizing public concern" around poverty, social and environmental issues. There are evidences that, when people at the grassroots level get organized either on their own or through the NGOs, they can fully in development programmes as active subjects and no more remain a passive and silent spectator of the fruits of the programmes.

Turning to the literature on economic development, the first half of the 1980s witnessed a subtle but significant shift in emphasis toward a more 'Free market' and "Participatory approach" to development. And yet within the third world itself, there were called for restructuring of the economic approach and models so that they may bring hope to hundreds of people struggling with the poverty, inequality, unemployment, population increase, over urbanization, public sector inefficiencies and to survive and preserve some hope that their situation might be changed. Thus the present state of economic development in developing countries calls a re-conceptualization of the current strategies which obviously demands for a new vision. Poverty continued to persist, with a large number of people being trapped below the poverty line. There is a steady erosion of the nature resource base. External dependence has consistently increased. As a consequence, questions of the relevance of the development paradigm are being raised, and limitation of the "Techno-economic" approach to development is being increasingly realized. Earlier it was assumed that rapid economic growth in developing countries could take place through central planning and regulation of the economy with emphasis on industrialization, modernization and urbanization. Marginal reform attempts aimed at welfare programmes and delivered inputs and only limited effects. Such limited attempts aimed at improving the efficiency of the delivery system did not produce expected results. It was therefore; felt that a new strategy was required.

Further, there was a major concern with the unsatisfactory outcome of past development activities. Notwithstanding advances made in many areas, the countries still faced serious and urgent problems of deep-rooted poverty, under employment, unemployment, waste of human resources, and under-utilization of manpower, and most importantly, growing majority's inability to meet their basic minimum needs. Under these conditions, it has become essential to redesign the existing programmes and target specific policies to the deprived section. If the past economic growth left these groups unaffected and in some instances even worsened, resulting in deterioration in the levels of living of those people, a frontal attack on poverty to help people meet their basic needs must, therefore, be given the maximum priority overall other types of developmental objectives and activities. However, this is easier said than done, given the experiences of the past three to four decades. In spite of various advantages offered by modern technology and international assistance, then has been very little success in elimination of mass poverty, destitution and impoverishment. If the fulfillment of basic need is the primary issue behind development, in developing countries it is essential to strengthen, mobilize and develop all possible sources of action. In particular, it is necessary to create an environment in which the people in each area can and will increasingly develop and mobilize their capacity to solve their own problems and build up their resource potential. Non-governmental organization can play a major role in providing this new impetus to development if they can be mobilized on nation side level. The compulsions to seek alternative driving forces for social change are mounting.

In the past, government intervention has at times led to the erosion of peoples effective participation in the overall development process. In recent years there are certain evidences that, when the people at the grassroot levels were organized through the process of social mobilization with active involvement of NGOs' in their own programmes, their effective participation in development process as actors rather than as passive objects of the process. They are able to move out of a condition of dehumanization and bare survival, to a position of systematic economic strength within a framework of people centered development. They have also proved capable of increasing saving, and engaging in income generating activities which not only enhanced their economic and social condition and dignity but also led to improvement in health and nutritional status of the vulnerable and disadvantaged groups such as the women and rural youth.

Active participation by Non-governmental organizations (NGOs) in developmental activities all over the world, particularly in the developing countries, is one of the most encouraging treads in the recent development experience. The entry of NGOs in development process represents an important response to the needs resulted due to the overburdened governments, the hesitant private sector and underutilized changes in the spectrum of NGO activities. Their traditional roles in welfare and service programmes are being strongly supplemented with many developmental activities. Not only have they been successful in filling up a critical institutional vacuum, but they have also demonstrated their overall effectiveness in working with poorer groups, in finding low-cost solutions, in improving the sue of local resources, and in encouraging self-reliance. Largely free of bureaucratic constraints, for testing new ideas and technologies and for mobilizing the community. They have developed durable partnership with both the government and the local people and, probably the most important of all, they have through their catalytic roles provided a ray of hope to people who would have never dreamt of gaining access to basic services and opportunities.

The most attractive aspects of NGO in the context of developmental programmes are some of the special features seen as critical factors in the process of socio-economic development. These characteristics, although not informally dividend in all NGOs, have been seen by many as an alternative model of development in developing countries with labour, scarce capital, and land resources, and a long history of centralized structures of decision making.

NGOs have relatively been more successful in organizing the rural poor, under specific programmes, than the government. This is so mainly because their programmes are specifically targeted; there is a strong component of local resources mobilization; and local organizations are encouraged to actively participate in the programme. Equally significant is the element of low-cost solutions that are deliberately selected so that local management and support will not be difficult. What emerges clearly from NGOs' experience is the extent to which rural poor are organized is not simple determined by creating a formal organizational mechanism, but also by choice of technology, the manner in which available resources are used, and the extent to which NGOs can and do maintain contact with the people are follow-up and project monitoring mechanisms. Obviously their overall commitment toward the poorer start of society is highly significant.

Many NGOs in the developing countries have demonstrated their capacities for organizing and undertaking innovative experiments and creating what might be called new approaches to development. In fact, they are of the greatest value for the alleviation of poverty. Breakthrough have been made in many cases for raising income levels for the poor, for protecting the environment and for launching programmes of support for the deprived, the disabled and the disadvantaged and for the women and the rural youth. Such innovative NGOs are, however, still limited in number and scope. Pioneering efforts need to be carefully assessed and the experiences be widely exchanged. In this way, better designed action projects at the grassroots could be developed by different NGOs in their respective areas and domains.

In almost all the successful NGOs programmes, it is almost certain that the prime determining factors are the roles of the committed NGO cadres in demonstrating leadership encouraging participation, displaying problem solving skills, and probably the most important, a willingness to work with the people. Given the complex dimensions of anti-poverty programme, the critical factor is not only the soundness of programmes that reflect the needs and interests of the peoples, but also their ability to create special cadres for their implementation. It is important for every NGO willing to participate in poverty alleviation programmes to see how such cadres can be developed. This can be the single most important factor to the programmes run by government bureaucracies, and yet the difficulties underlying the development of a large number of specially trained cadres for development works cannot be underestimated. There are questions of training, motivation, and future opportunities for such cadres, third world countries witnessed very encouraging success in its National Development Service (NDS). Small Farmers Development Programme (SFDP), Production Credit for Rural Women (PCRW) and various other community Development Programmes. These lessons are certainly very vital for the successful NGOs' entry into the poverty alleviation programme.

Successful experimentation in rural development, particularly in working with the groups, is relatively a new experience for many institutions. There are no typical models that can be emulated for widely differing environments. It is, therefore, highly pertinent that programmes are closely monitored and a certain amount of flexibility be built into it so that changes and follow ups can be regularly undertaken. Many NGOs programmes have such flexibilities which several governmental programmes conspicuously lack.

It would be appropriate to identify some of the apparent shortcomings evident in the NGO strategies. These shortcomings are especially relevant in the context of anti-poverty prgorammes that are generally seen in their scope and coverage and, type activities managed by NGOs. Many NGOs, even some of the largest ones, perceived their roles to be limited into the peripheral areas. They seldom have a clear strategic focus, often lack technical capability, and seem reluctant to cooperate with other organizations. The major constraints relate to:

By the very nature of their orientation, NGOs have had a tendency to function as distinct entities, each concerned mainly with its own problems. There have been too few contracts even between organizations working in similar areas and too little opportunity exist to learn from one another. Such isolated effort will not be sufficient to make meaningful breakthroughs in reducing the intensity of rural poverty if the NGOs, irrespective of their size of activity, would continue their work in isolated forms. They should, therefore, endeavor to line up their collective strength and resources to give mutual support to one another, either functionally in terms of various programmes of spatially in terms of areas of coverage, so that the results of the NGOs activities could be effective.

While many NGOs have demonstrated commendable roles in developing various technical package programmes for rural development problems, a large number of NGOs are still engaged primarily in the distributional role of various types of products in rural areas. Important as it is, this type of role is clearly insufficient. More effort has to be made to provide technically sound solutions to the different rural development problems. In this respect, the NGOs could function as effective media for dissemination of information on technical know-how, especially suitable for rural areas.

The process of development can no longer be tackled in isolation. It has a national dimension as well as international ones. A cohesive and sustainable development strategy is the rural order of the day within which a meaning balance between the Government and NGO sector should be reflected and a supplemental but essential role for international organizations be outlined. The challenge is to identify the transitional path that would enable one to bridge the gap between the current crisis and sustainable development. A policy framework for the collaboration of GO-NGO at both macro and sect oral planning and programming levels, has to be articulated in a way that can respond to the problems of deep-rooted poverty, unemployment, underemployment, malnutrition, waste of human resources and underutilized manpower. The same collaboration should also be maintained during implementation. This would mean a framework where growth, human development, and equity are taken as complementary and reinforcing elements.

Collective efforts in the mobilization sensitization and mass organization at all levels are needed and coherence has to be maintained. A national mechanism for dialogue between GO-NGO and implementation framework has to be evolved.

Recent events have shown that people centred development is a key and priority issue for the developing nations. For the NGOs whose charter and mission assigns to it the major responsibility empowering the people, enhancing the quality of life and human development by promoting social and economic development, a key challenge today is the need for an integrated approach. This involves bringing together the requirements of development, integrating development policies.

This leads to a new dimension in the co-operations of NGOs towards the creation of an atmosphere whereby the role of the NGO sector in development of broad Government policy, will continue to operate independently in response to the needs of the people.

United Nations has recognized the need of global partnership in development and empowerment of people with major role on collaboration between the government, International organizations and Non-governmental organizations. He emphasized the "need to push for a global partnership to promote the integration of the developing countries, and those in transition, into the world economy. International financial and developmental agencies are a powerful instrument for realizing a people centred vision of development that goes beyond the statistics of economic performance among the industrialized and the developing countries." He states that in turn it requires the empowerment of people in civil society, providing help where it needed by supporting indigenous communities, non-governmental organization, citizen's group and the private sector.

The NGO sector is larger and more complex than all the State networks combined. As such, it is a logistical fallacy that the State network alone can reach out to the critical mass of this world-the poor and the deprived – with viable measures of social welfare programme. The people themselves can and must reach out to themselves. This social geography lends enough to justification for the NGOs to lend their assistance to the people to lift themselves up.

1.5 Characteristics, Classification and Field Activities of NGOs

After discussing the relevant parameters of NGOs definition in the context of their varied activities over new issues and interest in the existing socio-economic and changed political situations, it would be now appropriate to highlight the characteristics, classifications and field activities of NGOs and their strengths and the weaknesses for taking a more holistic and sustainable long-term approach towards nurturing and supporting national development at the grass root level.

The literature on the various characteristics, classifications and the field activities of NGOs is vast and growing but varies in their legal status, functional category and sect oral involvement in terms of their activities, objectives and political orientation". Over the year, Non-Governmental Organizations include a wide variety of groups and institutions which differentiate them from other development organization. Indeed, these organizations are entirely or largely independent of government, and are characterized primarily by humanitarian or co-operative rather than commercial objectives. But due to basic reliance of these organizations on voluntary funding and small scale grass roots development project, the vast majority of development NGOs is quite small. However, they exert pressure to do more development work with small resources at their command particularly with local groups and individuals. These basic considerations have made these organizations certain theoretical characteristics which provide significant advantages as well as disadvantages in respect to operational activities.

The following basic theoretical considerations are felt to have certain significant operational advantages:

(i) As the organizations are small and informal, they can respond quickly and directly to development or humanitarian needs and opportunities.

(ii) NGOs can provide grass roots services and dynamism in poor communities in remote areas where the government and other development organization find it difficult to reach.

(iii) The basic responsiveness of NGOs is associated with special, cultural and other aspects of development which are generally ignored by the technical development specialists.

(iv) NGOs already have considerable experience in supporting the strategies, programmes and projects for both the rural and urban majority of poor.

(v) NGOs can help not only in identifying the community needs but also in mobilizing broad and active participation and support for local development activities.

(vi) NGOs have willingness to innovate new development approach, techniques, and experiments which may eventually prove quite significant in the context of broader development activities.

(vii) The operational activities of NGOs are fundamentally related to low overhead, cost on salaries, volunteers and appropriate technologies which make the formulated programmes of NGOs at low cost than the official programmes because they are committed to sustainable development approaches and to making more use of local resources.

Besides, those advantages, NGOs are felt to have the following operational disadvantages:

(i) Due to diverse variety of NGOs and their small scale and disparate aims and operational activities, many NGOs find it difficult to collaborate with other developmental organizations.

(ii) The informal and voluntary nature and scare resources generally create the problem of weak management of these organizations which can lead to a lack of control over operations and limited accountability for funds.

(iii) It is generally observed that activities of NGO are often individual efforts, implemented without a broader strategy, long term focus, or relationship to work with others institutions.

(iv) Some NGOs operate on the basis of political or religious objectives which can considerable hamper their work with government and other developmental organizations.

(v) NGOs can drift away from the innovation, flexibility, independence, and voluntary and participative spirit which actually made them successful in the first place owing to inappropriate support from governmental and multilateral agencies.

Scholars have tried to classify NGO according to their typology and sectoral involvement and this has direct relevance to programming for development. The major classifications are:

(i) Relief and Charity;

(ii) Development;

(iii) Mobilization and Organization;

(iv) Politics; and

(v) Political Education

In his study "From Relief To People's Movements" (1990), David Korten has classified the pattern of evaluation of NGOs under four generations. Viz.,

(i) Relief and welfare,

(ii) Community Development;

(iii) Sustainable Development;

(iv) People's Movements.

First generation strategies involve the NGO in the direct delivery of services to meet an immediate deficiency or shortage experienced by the beneficiary population, such as needs for food, health care or shelter. This generation strategies grow out of a long history of international voluntary action aimed at assisting the victims of wars and natural disasters, and providing welfare services to the poor.

Second generation strategies highlight the energies of the NGO on developing the capacities of the People to better meet their own needs through self-reliant local action which involves an implicit theory of village development in realizing it's own

Table-1.1: Strategies of Development–oriented NGOS: Four Generations

	Generation			
	First	*Second*	*Third*	*Fourth*
	Relief and Welfare	Community Development	Sustainable System Development	People's Movement
Problem Definition	Shortage	Local inertia	Institutional and Policy Constraints	Inadequate Mobilizing Vision
Time Frame	Immediate	Project Life	Ten to Twenty Years	Indefinite Future
Scope	Individual Or Family	Neighbourhood or Village	Region or Nation	National or Global
Chief Actors	NGO	NGO plus Community	All Relevant Public and Private Institutions	Loosely Defined Networks of People & Organizations
NGO Role	Doer	Mobilizer	Catalyst	Activist/Educator
Management Orientation	Logistics Management	Project Management	Strategic Management	Coalescing and Energizing self-Managing Networks
Development Education	Starving Children	Community Self-help	Constraining Policies and Institution	Spaceship Earth

(Source: David C. Korten, Getting to the twenty first Century : Voluntary Action and Global Agenda, Kumarian Press, West Hartford Connecticut, USA, 1990, p.10.)

potentials through education, organization, successful participation in activities, usually either a village or some subgroup within it, such as the women, or the landless agricultural workers.

Third generation strategies look beyond the individual community and seek changes in specific policies and institutions at local, national and global levels. This generation strategies focus attention on creating a policy and institutional setting that facilitates sustainable and inclusive local development in collaboration with major national agencies in helping and reorienting their policies and broadly-based local control over resources.

Fourth generation strategy focus attention on an inadequate mobilizing vision as the casual factor behind the present crisis facing both the developed and developing countries. It calls for imbuing the public consciousness with an alternative action. Plan for adequately mobilizing voluntary action on a national or global scale.

Table-1.2: Comparison of IDS (1985) and PACT (1987) Studies

	Ids (1985)		*Pact (1987)*
I.	Socio-Cultural	I.	Social Service
a.	Social/Cultural/religious Groups	a.	Social Service delivery
II.	Community Services	II.	Transitional
a.	Integrate community services	a.	Social services, equally mixed service delivery + development promotion
III.	Economic	III.	Developmental
a.	Asset Creation groups	a.	Local development promotion only.
b.	Labour exchange groups	b.	Sustainable local development promotion only.
c.	Credit exchange groups	c.	Sustainable and Geographically extendable development promotion.

The above four generations relating to the strategies of NGOs can be explained on the basis of the Table-1.1.

Besides these observations, there are two studies namely IDS (1985) and PACT (1987) which provide different functional categories of NGOs according to their typology and sectoral involvement in the context of the Nepalese economy. The IDS classification includes three such types, viz., Socio-cultural community services and economic. The PACT classification, on the other hand, represents an operational continuum with social Service as isolate, social service development promotion as transitional, and the last three exclusively developmental

A third study SAP-Nepal (1988) which has used accountability as the main criterion recognized only two categories of NGOs such as service NGOs and self-help NGOs. This typological division of NGOs is based on the growth sequence of the NGOs in Nepal which is given in the Table 1.3.

Table-1.3: Typological Division of NGOs

A. Sequence	*B. Type*	*C. Example*
Early	1. Social Welfare	Philanthropic, Relief
	2. Sectoral	Health, Education
	3. Community Development	Rural Development
Intermediate	4. Income generation	User groups
	5. Research & Development	PRDOs
Recent	6. Target-oriented	Women, Children
	7. Issue-oriented	Population, Environment
	8. Activist groups	Human rights

1.6.0 What Is Social Development?

Social development theory attempts to explain qualitative changes in the structure and framework of society, that help the society to better realize its aims and objectives. Development can be broadly defined in a manner applicable to all societies at all historical periods as an upward ascending movement featuring greater levels of energy, efficiency, quality, productivity, complexity, comprehension, creativity, mastery, enjoyment and accomplishment. Development is a process of social change, not merely a set of policies and programmes instituted for some specific results. This process has been going on since the dawn of history. But during the last five centuries it has picked up in speed and intensity, and during the last five decades has witnessed a marked surge in acceleration.

The basic mechanism driving social change is increasing awareness leading to better organization. Life evolves by consciousness and consciousness in turn progresses by organization. When society senses new and better opportunities for progress it accordingly develops new forms of organization to exploit these new openings successfully. The new forms of organization are better able to harness the available social energies and skills and resources to use the opportunities to get the intended results.

Development is governed by many factors that influence the results of developmental efforts. There must be a motive that drives the social change and essential preconditions for that change to occur. The motive must be powerful enough to overcome obstructions that impede that change from occurring. Development also needs resources such as capital and technology and the availability of supporting infrastructures.

- Development is the result of society's capacity to organize human energies and productive resources in order to meet the challenges and opportunities that life presents society with all the times. Society passes through well-defined stages in the course of its development. They are nomadic hunting and gathering, rural agrarian, urban, commercial, industrial and post-industrial societies. Pioneers introduce new ideas, practices and habits etc which are resisted in the beginning by the conservative element in society. At a later stage the innovations are accepted, imitated, organized and made use of by other members of the community. The organizational improvements introduced to support the innovations can take place

Table-1.4: Social Development Strategy

Areas of Action	*Link to the Sustainable Economic Growth Strategy*	*Link to the Poverty Reduction Strategy*
C. Promote Social Inclusion and Prevent Social Ills	Social Capital Development	Social Exclusion elimination by the generation of social capital
Objective: Social Capital Development and Social Inclusion of the excluded groups	Objective : Social Capital Development	Objective Integrate the excluded for better social development opportunities.
Sub-section :	Action :	Action :
(a) Information	• Promote information research and policies to attend discrimination.	• Monitor progress among excluded groups.
(b) Legislation	• Develop legislation to combat sigma and discrimination.	• Guarantee access to opportunities for the poor and excluded.

(*Contd.*)

(Contd. Table 1.4)

Areas Of Action	*Link to the Sustainable Economic Growth Strategy*	*Link to the Poverty Reduction Strategy*
(c) Institutions	• Incorporate social inclusion in policy analysis and national plans.	• Strengthen institutions to promote social inclusion.
(d) Labour markets and exclusion	• Promote efficient labour markets intermediation.	• Integrate labour markets with social and cultural features for excluded.
(e) Prevent social ills	• Reduction of economic losses generated by social ills.	• Prevent social and domestic violence and the spread of HIV/AIDS in poorest groups.
	Local levels, Local economics and Social Development	Local and territorial levels as locus for poverty reduction

(Contd.)

(Contd. Table 1.4)

Areas of Action	*Link to the Sustainable Economic Growth Strategy*	*Link to the Poverty Reduction Strategy*
Objective : Integrate Social Development Programs at Local Levels.	Objective: Social and economic development at local areas.	Objective: Target interventions to the poor at local level.
Subsections :	Actions :	Actions :
a) Neighborhood upgrading	• Improve infrastructure for urban population.	• Integrated packages of physical infrastructure for the poor neighborhoods.
b) Integrated community development projects	• Promote integration of isolated communities.	• Increase social economic development of indigenous, afro descendents and rural communities.

simultaneously at four different levels—physical, social, mental and psychological. Moreover, four different types of resources are involved in promoting development. Of these four, physical resources are the most visible but the least capable of expansion. The productivity of resources increases enormously as the quality of organization and level of knowledge inputs rise.

In sociology, the rise of social movements has been extensively examined in the context of national vs global movements (Minkoff, 1997; Tehranian, 1998; Ericson and Doyle, 1999), the impact and relevance for the private sector (Davis and Thompson, 1994; Grossman, 2000), and the role of social movements within institutional environments (Sjostrand, 1992). Historically, wide-ranging social movements - whether religious, cultural, or ethnic have called on governments and businesses to respond to dispersed societal interests. Often, government and business institutions have not addressed these interests until too late, and war or violent change has forced their incorporation. In other instances, such movements were simply suppressed. Citizens' growing loss of trust in institutions they rely upon to protect interests of social import has fanned a need for new mechanisms to foster social capital formation that Putnam would describe as 'outward looking' and 'bridging' (Putnam, 2002, 11). Davis and McAdam (2000), Rao et al. (2000), and Smith et al. (1997) all provide evidence that social movements are becoming more organized, influential, and integrated into global political and business systems, and often are assuming new organizational forms. When the interests embodied in a social movement evolve structurally to form a free-standing presence within the broader institutional environment, the resulting entity is termed an NGO. Not all social movements spawn NGOs; in some instances, however, prevalent institutional contexts favor the formalization of movements into NGOs through rules related to fundraising, access to representation within decision-making, and enhanced social legitimacy.

The major players in NGOs for social purpose are those who contribute time or resources to the organization; NGO staff, management, and board members who direct and monitor the organization's activities; and individuals, private foundations, governments, and multilateral institutions that provide funding support (donors). Social purpose NGOs are accountable to the 'clients' they serve - the objects of the social movement that gave rise to the NGO's formation - and their ultimate success is measured by their impact on these clients and their communities (Woller and Parsons, 2002). Examples of social purpose clients include people afflicted with HIV/ AIDS, ethnic minorities threatened with genocide, certain animal or plant species facing extinction, and women denied access to public services and opportunities for advancement. Figure 1 depicts another category of NGO that can result from collective action taken by individuals within society - the membership or 'club' NGO.2 Club theory within economics posits that agents form groups to confer externalities on one another (Buchanan, 1965): by joining forces, members can improve their own utility. Club NGOs share similarities with Putnam's 'inward-looking' social capital, which tends to promote the material, social, or political interests of their own members' (Putnam, 2002, 11). Club NGOs are reflective of relationships that have been characterized as 'solidaristic individualism' (Rothstein, 2002) and 'loose connections' (Wuthnow, 2002), and are viewed as 'narrower, less bridging, and less focused on ... public-regarding purpose' (Putnam, 2002, 412). Examples of club NGOs are unions, business associations, and church groups. Vakil (1997, 2057) suggests that 'lack of consensus on how to define and classify NGOs has inhibited progress on both the theoretical and empirical fronts in the effort to better understand and facilitate the functioning of the NGO sector.

Social development means transforming institutions to empower people. Empowering People by Transforming Institutions by promoting equal access to opportunities, enabling everyone to contribute to social and economic progress and share in its rewards and addressing common needs, overcoming constraints and considering diverse interests. AmartyaSen (2002) not only emphasizes the importance of assets but draws attention to their returns—how those assets translate into improved well-being for poor people. To ensure those returns, institutions must allow assets to be used productively and freely, promoting what Sen calls capabilities. Similarly, the sustainable livelihoods framework identifies five asset classes as important for well-being and livelihoods: physical, financial, human, natural and social. Institutions determine how these assets improve livelihoods.

The 1995 Copenhagen Summit on Social Development pledged to "make the conquest of poverty, the goal of full employment and the fostering of stable, safe and just societies" their overriding objectives, making the following commitments:

Commitment 1: Enabling environment for social development

Commitment 2: Poverty eradication

Commitment 3: Full employment

Commitment 4: Social integration

Commitment 5: Gender equity

Commitment 6: Basic services and promotion of culture

Commitment 7: Accelerated development of Africa and the least developed countries

Commitment 8: Including social dimensions in structural adjustment

Commitment 9: Increasing resources for social development

Commitment 10: Strengthening cooperation for social development

In 2000, the Millennium Development Declaration underlines the importance of social development, basing the MDGs on "certain fundamental values essential to international relations in the twenty-first century." These include:

Freedom: Men and women have the right to live their lives and raise their children in dignity, free from hunger and from the fear of violence, oppression or injustice. Democratic and participatory governance: Based on the will of the people best assures these rights.

Equality: No individual and no nation must be denied the opportunity to benefit from development. The equal rights and opportunities of women and men must be assured.

Solidarity: Global challenges must be managed in a way that distributes the costs and burdens fairly in accordance with basic principles of equity and social justice.

Tolerance: Human beings must respect one another, in all their diversity of belief, culture and language.

Social development transforms societies by understanding the social context of the country as well as the needs and priorities of poor people. Poor people's own voices tell us that poverty is more than low income - it is also about vulnerability, exclusion and isolation, poor governance, and powerlessness. People's priorities and experiences are affected by such variables as gender, social exclusion, intra-household allocation of resources, incidence of crime and violence, geographical location, access to networks of support, and relations with those in power. By capturing different dimensions of poverty, a multidisciplinary approach can deepen our understanding of poverty and the lives of the poor.

As such, social development aims to promote the transformation of subjects and beneficiaries into citizens by fostering an enabling, accessible, responsive, and accountable state. This requires:

- policies that recognize and advance the universal rights and responsibilities of citizens, and strengthen the capacity of citizens to claim their rights;
- a recognition and celebration of multiculturalism as a source of strength for societies;
- support for policies that accommodate diversity in the achievement of universal rights; and,
- an understanding of the role of power relations, and the importance of creating institutional mechanisms that offer redress against power inequities.

1.7 NGOs and Social Development

The phrase "non-governmental organization (NGO)" came into use in 1945 with the establishment of provisions in Article 71 of Chapter 10 of the United Nations Charter for a consultative role for organizations that are neither governments nor member states. Globalization during the 20th century gave rise to the importance of NGOs. Many problems could not be solved within a nation. International treaties and international organizations such as the World Trade Organization were perceived as being too centered on the interests of capitalist enterprises. In an attempt to counterbalance this trend, NGOs have developed to emphasize humanitarian issues, developmental aid and sustainable development.

Three stages or generations of NGO evolution have been identified by Korten's (1990) *Three Generations of Voluntary Development Action*. First, the typical development NGO focuses on relief and welfare, and delivers relief services directly to beneficiaries. Examples are the distribution of food, shelter or health services. The NGO notices immediate needs and responds to them. NGOs in the second generation are oriented towards small-scale, self-reliant local development. At this evolutionary stage, NGOs build the capacities of local communities to meet their needs through 'self reliant local action'. Korten calls the third generation 'sustainable systems development'. At this stage, NGOs try to advance changes in policies and institutions at a local, national and international level; they move away from their operational service providing role towards a catalytic role. The NGO is starting to develop from a relief NGO to a development NGO.

The primary purpose of an operational NGO is the design and implementation of development-related projects. One categorization that is frequently used is the division into 'relief-oriented' or 'development-oriented' organizations; they can also be classified according to whether they stress service delivery or participation; or whether they are religious and secular; and whether they are more public or private-oriented. Operational NGOs can be community-based, national or international.

NGOs exist for a variety of purposes, usually to further the political or social goals of their members or funders. Examples include improving the state of the natural environment, encouraging the observance of human rights, improving the welfare of the disadvantaged, or representing a corporate agenda. However, there are a huge number of such organizations and their goals cover a broad range of political and philosophical positions. This can also easily be applied to private schools and athletic organizations.

Non-governmental organizations (NGOs) have played a major role in pushing for sustainable development at the international level. Campaigning groups have been key drivers of inter-governmental negotiations, ranging from the regulation of hazardous wastes to a global ban on land mines and the elimination of slavery.

But NGOs are not only focusing their energies on governments and inter-governmental processes. With the retreat of the state from a number of public functions and regulatory activities, NGOs have begun to fix their sights on powerful corporations - many of which can rival entire nations in terms of their resources and influence. Aided by advances in information and communications technology, NGOs have helped to focus attention on the social and environmental externalities of business activity. Multinational brands have been acutely susceptible to pressure from activists and from NGOs eager to challenge a company's labor, environmental or human rights record. Even those businesses that do not specialize in highly visible branded goods are feeling the pressure, as campaigners develop techniques to target downstream customers and shareholders.

Social development theory attempts to explain qualitative changes in the structure and framework of society that help the society to better realize its aims and objectives. Development can be broadly defined in a manner applicable to all societies at all historical periods as an upward ascending movement featuring greater levels of energy, efficiency, quality, productivity, complexity, comprehension, creativity, mastery, enjoyment and accomplishment. Development is a process of social change, not merely a set of policies and programs instituted for some specific results. This process has been going on since the dawn of history. But during the last five centuries it has picked up in speed and intensity, and during the last five decades has witnessed a marked surge in acceleration.

The basic mechanism driving social change is increasing awareness leading to better organization. Life evolves by consciousness and consciousness in turn progresses by organization. When society senses new and better opportunities for progress it accordingly develops new forms of organization to exploit these new openings successfully. The new forms of organization are better able to harness the available social energies and skills and resources to use the opportunities to get the intended results.

Development is governed by many factors that influence the results of developmental efforts. There must be a motive that drives the social change and essential preconditions for that change to occur. The motive must be powerful enough to overcome obstructions that impede that change from occurring. Development also needs resources such as capital and technology and the availability of supporting infrastructures.

Development is the result of society's capacity to organize human energies and productive resources in order to meet the challenges and opportunities that life presents society with all the times. Society passes through well-defined stages in the course of its development. They are nomadic hunting and gathering, rural agrarian, urban, commercial, industrial and post-industrial societies. Pioneers introduce new ideas, practices and habits etc which are resisted in the beginning by the conservative element in society. At a later stage the innovations are accepted, imitated, organized and made use of by other members of the community. The organizational improvements introduced to support the innovations can take place simultaneously at four different levels—physical, social, mental and psychological. Moreover four different types of resources are involved in promoting development. Of these four, physical resources are the most visible but the least capable of expansion. The productivity of resources increases enormously as the quality of organization and level of knowledge inputs rise.

The pace and scope for development varies according to the stage that society is enduring the developmental process. The three main stages are physical, vital (the term vital refers to the dynamic and nervous social energies of humanity that propel individuals to accomplish) and mental and all these three have their own unique characteristics.

Social movements and NGOs have the collective action of a group of individuals is sustained over time in an identifiable way and reflects an important emerging social change, it is termed a social movement. The civil rights movement in the United States and the global human rights movement are examples of this phenomenon. In sociology, the rise of social movements has been extensively examined in the context of national vs global movements (Minkoff, 1997; Tehranian, 1998; Ericson and Doyle, 1999), the impact and relevance for the private sector (Davis and Thompson, 1994; Grossman, 2000), and the role of social movements within institutional environments (Sjostrand, 1992). Historically, wide- ranging social movements - whether religious, cultural, or ethnic have called on governments and businesses to respond to dispersed societal interests. Often, the government and business institutions have not addressed these interests until too late, and war or violent change has forced their incorporation.

In other instances, such movements were simply suppressed. Citizens' growing loss of trust in institutions they rely upon to protect interests of social import has fanned a need for new mechanisms to foster social capital formation that Putnam would describe as 'outward looking' and 'bridging' (Putnam, 2002, 11). Davis and McAdam (2000), Rao et al. (2000), and Smith et al. (1997) all provide evidence that social movements are becoming more organized, influential, and integrated into global political and business systems, and often are assuming new organizational forms. When the interests embodied in a social movement evolve structurally to form a free-standing presence within the broader institutional environment, the resulting entity is termed an NGO. Not all social movements spawn NGOs; in some instances, however, prevalent institutional contexts favour the formalization of movements into NGOs through rules related to fundraising, access to representation within decision-making, and enhanced social legitimacy. In these settings, formal NGO formation mitigates important obstacles to the sustenance of collective action. Journal of International Business Studies:

The importance of non-governmental organizations HildyTeegen et al 466 NGOs arising from social movements are describe as 'social purpose NGOs' and include environmental groups and human rights organizations. The major players in social purpose NGOs are: individuals who contribute time or resources to the organization; NGO staff, management, and board members who direct and monitor the organization's activities; and individuals, private foundations, governments, and multilateral institutions that provide funding support (donors). Social purpose NGOs are accountable to the 'clients' they serve - the objects of the social movement that gave rise to the NGO's formation - and their ultimate success is measured by their impact on these clients and their communities (Woller and Parsons, 2002). Examples of social purpose clients include people afflicted with HIV/ AIDS, ethnic minorities threatened with genocide, certain animal or plant species facing extinction, and women denied access to public services and opportunities for advancement.

This depicts another category of NGO that can result from collective action taken by individuals within society - the membership or 'club' NGO.2 Club theory within economics posits that agents form groups to confer externalities on one another (Buchanan, 1965): by joining forces, members can improve their own utility. Club NGOs share similarities with Putnam's 'inward-looking' social capital, which 'tend(s) to promote the material, social, or political interests of their own members' (Putnam, 2002, 11). Club NGOs are reflective of relationships that have been characterized as 'solidaristic individualism' (Rothstein, 2002) and 'loose connections' (Wuthnow, 2002), and are viewed as 'narrower, less bridging, and less focused on ... public-regarding purpose' (Putnam, 2002, 412). Examples of club NGOs are unions, business associations, and church groups. Vakil (1997, 2057) suggests that 'lack of consensus on how to define and classify NGOs has inhibited progress on both the theoretical and empirical fronts in the effort to better understand and facilitate the functioning of the NGO sector.' The acronym NGO is not very helpful in describing the organizations it defines, in that it tells us what the organizations are not, rather than what they are. The term 'NGO' dates from 1950, when the United Nations coined the expression (Vakil, 1997, 2068). Presumably the UN, which dealt primarily with governments and wanted to consult private, non-profit organizations that were independent of governments, found it convenient to refer to them simply as NGOs to distinguish them from governments.

Today the United Nations (2003) describes an NGO as follows: any non-profit, voluntary citizens' group which is organized on a local, national or international level. Task-oriented and driven by people with a common interest, NGOs perform a variety of services and humanitarian functions, bring citizens' concerns to Governments, monitor policies and encourage political participation at the community level. They provide analysis and expertise, serve as early warning mechanisms and help monitor and implement international agreements. Some are organized around specific issues, such as human rights, the environment or health. In the remainder of this article, we focus on social purpose NGOs (referring to them simply as 'NGOs') and define them as follows: NGOs are private, not-for-profit organizations that aim to serve particular societal interests by focusing advocacy and/ or operational efforts on social, political and economic goals, including equity, education, health, environmental protection and human rights. Having defined NGOs as the organizational manifestations of civil society interests, we now discuss the role and function of NGOs relative to their public- and private-sector counterparts (governments and firms, respectively) in value creation and governance globally. We also highlight the way their roles and activities serve to classify them.

1.7.1 Multidimensional Poverty Index: Basic Overview

The MPI is an index of acute multidimensional poverty. It reflects deprivations in very rudimentary services and core human functions for people across 104 countries. Although deeply constrained by data limitations, the MPI reveals a different pattern of poverty than income poverty, as it illuminates a different set of deprivations. The MPI has three dimensions: health, education, and standard of living. These are measured using ten indicators. Poor households are identified and an aggregate measure constructed using the methodology proposed by Alkire and Foster (2007,2009). Each dimension is equally weighed; each indicator within a dimension is also equally weighed.

The MPI reveals the combination of deprivations that better a household at the same time. A household is identified as multidimensionally poor if, and only if, it is deprived in some combination of indicators are presented below:

A. Health :

Child Mortality : If any child has died in the family.

Nutrition : If any adult or child in the family is malnourished.

B. Education :

Years of Schooling: (If no household member has completed 5 years of schooling).

Child of Enrolment: (If any school-aged child is out of school in years 1 to 8).

C. Standard of Living :

Electricity (no electricity is poor)

Drinking Water (MDG definitions)

Sanitation (MDG definitions, including the toilet is not shared)

Flooring (dirt/sand/dung are poor)

Cooking Fuel (wood/charcoal/dung are poor)

Assets (poor if do not own more than one of: radio, tv, telephone, bike, motorbike)

The MPI is the product of two numbers: the Headcount H or percentage of people who are poor, and the Average Intensity of deprivation A – which reflects the proportion of dimensions in which households are deprived. Alkire and Foster show that this measure is very easy to calculate and interpret, is intuitive yet robust, and satisfies many desirable properties.

1.7.2 Millennium Development Goals (MDGs)

Since 2000, the United Nations and World Bank have compiled and reported data on the progress of nations and regions with respect to a uniform set of targets and indicators. These targets and indicators were agreed upon within the MDG framework, and countries progress towards them has been monitored. The additional quantitative targets are needed because income poverty measures provide vitally important but incomplete guidance to redress multidimensional poverty.

The MDGs catalyzed the collection and compilation of comparable international data related to the agreed goals and targets. The MDG statistics are presented annually and have been tremendously useful in providing feedback regarding improved development outcomes and in creating incentives to address core deprivations.

Unlike the MPI, however, the international MDG reports invariably report progress on each indicator singly. No composite MDG index has been developed, and few studies have reflected the interconnections between indicators. The reason that no composited MDG index has been developed is plain to see: the 'denominator' or base population of MDG indicators differ. In some cases it is all people (malnutrition, income); in some cases children (primary school, immunization), or youth 15-24 (literacy), or childbearing women (maternal mortality), or urban slum dwellers (housing), or households (access to secure tenure), and so on. Some environmental indicators do not refer to human populations at all. Given this diversity of indicators, it is difficult to construct an index meaningfully brings all deprivations into the same frame.

The Millennium Development Goals and targets come from the Millennium Declaration signed by 189 countries, including 147 Heads of State, in September 2000. The goals and targets are inter-related and should be seen as a whole. They represent a partnership between the developed countries and the developing countries determined, as the Declaration states, "to create an environment at the national and global levels alike-which is conducive to development and the elimination of poverty". The following are the major goals;

Goal 1: Eradicate extreme poverty and hunger

Goal 2: Achieve universal primary education

Goal 3: Promote gender equality and empower women

Goal 4: Reduce child mortality

Goal 5: Improve maternal health

Goal 6: Combat HIV/AIDS, malaria and other diseases

Goal 7: Ensure environmental sustainability

Goal 8: Develop a global partnership for development

1.7.3 Human Development Index of India(census 2010)

Human Development Index Rank	=	119
Human Development Index value	=	0.519
Life expectancy at birth (Years)	=	64.4
Mean Years of Schooling (Years)	=	4.4
Expected Years of Schooling (Years)	=	10.3
Gross National Income (GNI) per capita	=	3.337
GNI per capita rank minus HID rank	=	-6
Non-income HID value	=	0.549

1.8 NGOs and Social Responsibility

With changing times, the scope and area of "social development" is widening and deepening by the day. The existing social relations in societies based on injustice have been drawing protests. For this purpose, raising agendas of oppressed and exploited communities, making them conscious and pushing these agendas forward need awareness, organization and movements. Social organizations at this moment play a role of a pressure group. So, like volunteer work in the social development process, social upliftment craves for social movement. The NGOs have been responsible for addressing both these issues.

In reality, social development is not possible without social freedom. The issues of social justice and freedom could not go ahead without sacrifice and commitment. For this, people are required to develop a sense of service and sacrifice. So, the self-service is a basic ingredient of social development activity. Likewise, in order to end the pervasive exploitation and suppression in the society, social awareness and social mobilization should go hand in hand with volunteer attitude. 'Social activeness is another requirement in the social development sector. Similarly, committed, trained, and progressive human resources are imminent to let the area of social development go ahead with a clear vision, aim and program. Also, experts are required in this area. So, as it is necessary for it to be a social movement to push the social development issues, similarly it should be pro-awareness and change-oriented. Looking at the history of social service, we find the social development activity is always message-oriented. Therefore, social responsibilities of NGOs have become important for transforming the society (Pradhan 2003).

1.9 Involvement of NGOs in Various Sectors of Social Development

The NGOs engaged in social development have now been actively involving themselves in relief package and development along with other activities like resource mobilization, social mobilization, awareness, skill development and rehabilitation. Besides, the activities of social development have gradually been moving ahead in different projects like drinking water in villages, small hydropower, forest conservation, human rights, education and economic development sectors. So, it is difficult to confine the working areas of social developments. However, in the present context, studying the impacts and areas of social movement, it can be divided into the following categories.

a. Area linked with relief and welfare (humanitarian aid)

b. Area linked with society and reform

c. Area linked with economic development and self-dependency (human resource development)

d. Village reconstruction area, etc. (Pradhan 2003).

The area of relief and welfare issues are mainly concerned with humanitarian services and assistance. Especially, people affected by raging conflict or natural disaster or fire need immediate humanitarian aid. Medicines, clothes, food, accommodation, psychological assistance, among others, are included in such services. The NGOs have been working to minimize the disaster by collecting relief materials, their transformation and distribution. Another important area of social development is the management of victims, meaning necessary relief, socialization and reform for children, women and men victimized by different exploitation, discrimination, disaster, punishment and criminal acts. For this purpose, efforts are on for the required psychosocial consultation on different matters and social reunification. For the people involved in addictions and crime also these organizations provide psychological consultations, and socialization and reform opportunities.

For centuries, responsible and aware members of the society have been conducting campaigns for social awareness and mobilization against social injustice, economic exploitation, and discrimination. During the course, it is quite obvious that the civil society, mainly social organizations and institutions have been playing pertinent roles. It is clear that non-government organizations in Nepal are - involved directly in different activities ranging from human rights, child-rights, women empowerment, and liberty to ethnic and suppressed class to ensuring of economic and cultural rights of the people. The social mobilization programs for strengthening human rights and democratic rights, against the anti-nationals, in aid of children and women, in response to sex trade, bondage and bonded-labourers are very important. It is also known to all that Nepali NGO movement advocated for democracy; freedom and change even during yesterday's undemocratic system's influence (Pradhan 2003).

Another important area of social development is an issue of economic development and self-dependency for poor and backward people. No matter how beautiful thoughts for social welfare are, they cannot be sustainable and dynamic unless they do not free the people from unemployment, labour-exploitation, and poverty. Like in other countries, programmes on poverty alleviation or poverty reduction are mobilized by the state in Nepal. They are also recognised as national priority. But, country's economic and social development is not possible unless employment creation, resource generating activities, and economic self-dependency programmes are not implemented effectively. In this context, several NGOs in the country have joined hands with local communities by involving in promoting micro-credit projects, rural bank, skilled education and employment programmes, fair trade, skill enhancement of women, agriculture and livestock, and other economic activities. The NGOs have been running campaigns for rights on resources, and have received some successes, as well.

People face immense difficulty in their livelihood, if schools, health centers, hospitals, community buildings, bridges, roads, communication facilities, and electricity and the like are not available. So, the NGOs are seriously involved in such type of village development and reconstruction. NGOs are engaged in construction and reconstruction works linked with education, health, agriculture, and social and economic issues as per the need of the poor and needy people in urban and rural areas.

1.10 NGOS and Sustainable Development

The NGOs, functions for the promotion of sustainable community development. Specifically,on microfinance, initiation of community capacity building and self reliance. Eventually, sustainable community development will be achieved, particularly when community is empowered. The 'bottom-up approach' in community development would likely bring about empowerment to the community and finally sustainable community development. According to Finger (1994), the bottom-up approach emphasizes community participation, grassroots movements and local decision making. It argues that community participation and grassroots initiatives promote participatory decision making and local self-reliance (Panda 2007). In bottom-up approach, people are able to define their own problems and having ability and capacity to solve it through organizing and participating themselves.

1.10.1 Microfinance and Development

During the 1990s, scholars have increasingly referred to microfinance as an effective means of poverty reduction (Rekha 1995; Cerven and Ghazanfar 1999; Pankhurst and Johnston 1999). Oxaal and Baden (1997). Mayoux (2000) and Cheston and Khan (2002) have pointed out the importance of microfinance in empowerment, particularly women empowerment. Microfinance is defined as efforts to improve the access to loans and to saving services for poor people (Shreiner 2001). It is currently being promoted as a key development strategy for promoting poverty eradication and economic empowerment. It has the potential to effectively address material poverty, the physical deprivation of goods and services and the income to attain them by granting financial services to households who are not supported by the formal banking sector (Sheration 2004). Microcredit programs provide small loans and savings opportunities to those who have traditionally been excluded from commercial financial services. As a development inclusion strategy, microfinance programs emphasize women's economic contribution as a way to increase overall financial efficiency within national economies.

According to Cheston and Khan (2002), one of the most popular forms of economic empowerment for women is microfinance, which provides credit for poor women who are usually excluded from formal credit institutions. Since the 1990s, microfinance institutions have addressed the issues of sustainability, participation and empowerment. These issues have been researched and debated by donor agencies, NGOs, feminists, and activists (Johnson and Rogaly 1997; Razavi 1997; Kabeer 1999; Mayoux 2001; Mahmud 2003). However, underneath these shared concerns lie three fundamentally different approaches to microfinance: financial sustainability, feminist empowerment, and poverty alleviation. All the three microfinance approaches have different goals coupled with varied perspectives on how to incorporate gender into microfinance policy and programs (Mayoux 2000).

The microfinance empowers women by putting capital in their hands and allowing them to earn an independent income and contribute financially to their household and communities. This economic empowerment is expected to generate increased self-esteem, respect, and other forms of empowerment for women beneficiaries. Some evidence show that microfinance would empower women in some domains such as increased participation in decision making, more equitable status of women in the family and community, increased political power and rights, andincreased self-esteem (Cheston and Kuhn 2002). Well being as an output of microfinance not only covers the economic indicators, but also other indicators such as community education, environment, recreation and accessibility to social services. It is related to the quality of life (Asnarulkhadi 2002).

In order to gain economic sustainability, NGOs through microfinance help the communities to reduce poverty, create jobs, and promote income generation. In the developing countries, sustainability is linked more closely to issues of poverty and the gross inequalities of power and resources (Hamnett and Hassan 2003). This is due to the fact that in the Third World Countries, the ecological system sometimes conflicts with the socio-economic needs of local people who depend on a local ecosystem for their survival (Nygren 2000). In contrast, in the developed countries, as Bradshaw and Winn (2000) have noted, more priority is given on environmental aspect of sustainable development. In these countries, since the wealth of the nation and of most individuals has reached a certain level, therefore sustainability has been fueled primarily by concern for such issues as climate change, biodiversity, the deprivation of the natural environment, and the over-consumption of natural resources especially non-renewable (Hibbard and Chuntang 2004).

1.10.2 Capacity Building and Development

As mentioned earlier, capacity building is another NGO's strategy that helps to bring about sustainable community development. Capacity building is a approach to development that builds independence. It can be: A 'means to an end', where the purpose is for others to take on programs. An 'end' in itself, where the intent is to enable others, from individuals through to government departments, to have greater capacity to work together to solve problems. A process, where capacity building strategies are routinely incorporated as an important element of effective practice (NSW Health 2001).

Before beginning to build capacity within programs, practitioners need to identify pre-existing capacities such as skills, structures, partnerships and resources. Frankish (2003) has counted a number of dimensions for community capacity including financial capacity (resources, opportunities and knowledge), human resources (Skills, motivations, confidence, and relational abilities and trust) and social resources (networks, participation structures, shared trust and bonding).

UNDP (1997) has introduced capacity building as the process by which individuals, groups, and organizations increase their abilities to (1) perform core functions, solve problems, define and achieve objectives; and (2) understand and deal with their development needs in a broad context and in a sustainable manner. Furthermore, in terms of NGOs' functions, Langran (2002) has defined capacity building as the ability of one group (NGOs) to strengthen the development abilities of another group (local communities) through education, skill training and organizational support.

Capacity building is an approach to development not a set of pre-determined activities. There is no single way to build capacity. Although experience tells us that there is a need to work across the key action areas, practitioners approach each situation separately to identify pre-existing capacities and develop strategies particular to a program or organization, in its time and place. NGOs, through the provision of education, skill and knowledge, develop the capacity of community towards achieving sustainable development.

In fact, NGOs act as a capacity builder to help the community to develop the resources, building awareness, motivating to participation in project and finally improving the quality of community's lives. A link to empowerment is frequently cited as one of the reasons for and outcomes of community capacity building. Empowerment is discussed at the level of individual empowerment (changes in skills, knowledge, consciousness and awareness, hope, action and beliefs in abilities to effect change) and changes in wider social structures and processes that result in increased resources and opportunities (Verity 2007). Furthermore, with regards to sustainability, capacity building has been identified in much sustainable development policy as one of the key strategies for increasing the potential towards sustainable development. For example, in a program to train women to establish a small enterprise, a positive result will be that women have co-operated to start the enterprise, but a sustainable outcome will depend on whether women have the capacity to make it work and derive an income from it without external financial or technical assistance (Viswanath 1991). Many researchers argue that building community capacities and fostering empowerment are more effective ways of achieving sustainable community development than programs and success indicators imposed by outside experts (Harrison 1998; Mobbs 1998). They point out that outside experts usually have limited knowledge and understanding of the particular context, needs and issues of a community. Local solutions to achieving sustainable community and economic development are therefore seen as important outcomes of a capacity-building approach (Lennie 2005). For example, to increase the people's participation in order to achieve sustainable development, many issues should be considered, such as skills, leadership, knowledge, physical resources and stakeholder representativeness.

1.10.3 Self reliance and Development

Self reliance is another strategy that effects sustainable community development. Effective community development sits on the foundation of self-reliance. The concept of self reliance is strategically situated within the essence of community development and is related to other concepts like mutual help, self-help, participation of the indigenous people and rural progress. Self reliance encourages the necessity for people to use local initiatives, their abilities and their own possessions to improve their condition. Fonchingong and Fonjong (2002) have pointed out that self reliance is increasingly being adopted as modus operandi for community development. According to Kelly (1992), Self reliance means that the people rely on their own resources and are independent of funds sourced outside the community. Self reliant strategy relies on the willingness and ability of the local people to depend on their own available resources and technology which they can control and manage. A self reliant strategy requires the optional use of all available human, natural and technological resources (Agere 1982). Although dependence on the state may be desirable in the short term, it should not be a long term objective, because the aim of the community development must ultimately be self reliance. Reliance on external resources will lead to the loss of autonomy and independence of the community.

On the other hand, autonomous communities can flourish only in the absence of such external dependency. Therefore, to attain self reliance, community workers (e.g.NGOs) and community groups must discover their own potential and look for ways to innovatively develop such discovered potential to use as sources of wealth for the development of the community (Ife and Tesoriero 2006). Motivating and mobilizing people to be self reliant and to participate in development activities become an important objective of the NGOs. According to Korten (1990), the second strategy of the NGOs focuses on developing the capacities of the people to better meet their own needs through self-reliant local action. In the second generation strategy, Korten (1990), mentioned that the local inertia is the heart of problem in a village or community.

There is a potential energy in a community but remains inactive because of the inertia of tradition, isolation and lack of education. But this inertia can be broken through the intervention of an outside change agent (NGOs and other agents) who helps the community realize its potentials through education, organization, consciousness, raising small loans and the introduction of simple new technologies. It is the stress on local self reliance, with the intent that benefits will be sustained by community self help action beyond the period of NGO assistance (Korten 1990). Therefore, NGOs, through the strategy of self reliance, can facilitate sustainable development of the community.

In view of the brief introduction of the research study, it is focused on the policies and programs of government promoting inclusion of NGOs participation and a great deal of financial resources and human resources are in mission, it is more pertinent to study the contributions of these organizations for social development. Moreover, studying critically the policies and programs of functionaries and the perceptions of the beneficiaries will have a supreme significance in understanding the outcomes of deliberate efforts.

Professionalization of social organizations is one of the great concerns of India at the mode of development and therefore reviewing the professional standards of functionaries and the satisfaction of the beneficiaries of Social organizations become vital. Vizianagram is one of the backward districts and has become a place for several NGOs for launching their social development programs with the financial support of international and national organizations. The present study will highlight the significant contributions of these NGOs for the social development, their strategies and target groups, issues and problems and thereby enable the system to function effectively and efficiently. Such a study would also help in minimizing the wastage of resources.

As it is a backward district, the government has been promoting social development activities to uplift the social standards by extending cooperation with NGOs. There are several NGOs in the recent past have established their field offices and executing varieties of social development programs such as health, education, rural development, women welfare, child labor, etc., which are sponsored by .national as well as international agencies.

Chapter - II

Review Of Related Literature

2

Review of Related Literature

In this chapter, an attempt is made to present the review of related literature on the research study the contributions of NGOs for social development. It was felt necessary to acquire some information and insight into perspectives on NGO's and their contributions. When total monetary and human resources involved in social organizations are huge, it is more pertinent to study social organization from the point of view of their functionaries beneficiaries and infrastructure. Today we live in consumerist society in which consumer's satisfaction and delight are of tremendous value. The two consumers (one internal and one external) of NGO's are beneficiaries and functionaries. With these two human groups in the NGOs and along with their infrastructure would decide the presence and future of these NGOs. The beneficiaries of the social organizations are independent variable. It is because of them social organizations exist. Therefore it is essential to understand whether beneficiaries of the social organizations get effective, efficient and quality service or not.

In this chapter therefore a discussion is presented firstly on relevance of reviewing existing literature on the basis of major works in the field of development was evolved. Following are the studies conducted in the area of contribution of NGOs for social development.

2.1 Relevance of Reviewing Literature

The Review of Literature is pre-requisite for initiating any research work. Starting from the conceptualization to the completion of the research, concurrent review of literature helps researcher a lot in many ways. Review of Literature can sensitize researcher towards the topic and he can learn from the past as to what and how the theme of the research has been studied. Researcher can learn from the mistakes committed in the past. The review of literature helps researcher to prepare a background of theme of research and to identify the researchable problem with theoretical and conceptual framework of the study. It avoids futile duplications and satisfies intellectual curiosity after careful consideration of what has been done so far. Goode and Hatt contributed a major book title Methods in Social research (1952) in which they write "An important part of the preparation for research work consists in learning how to use the resource material. It is important because all research inevitably involves the use of book, pamphlet, periodical and documentary materials in libraries. This applies to studies based upon original data gathered in a field study as well as that base entirely upon documentary sources. In both types of studies, there is the same need for using certain basic kinds of published materials.

On the other hand, general source materials have to be consulted for the necessary background knowledge of the problem to be investigated; obviously, no research project can be undertaken without this preliminary orientation. Nor should one be undertaken without knowledge of the research that has already been done in the field. It provides further orientation to the problem and at the same time eliminates the possibility of unnecessary duplication of effort."

This discussion on review of literature throughout the research period justifies the need, relevance and substance of it at various stages of research.

2.2 Research Studies on NGOs and Their Contribution to Social Development

NGO's can be studied from various perspectives – their existence, their roles in society, their formation, their management, their criteria such as – kind of services/products they provide, people and areas they serve, people , the resources they mobilize and from where, their size and shape, their legal forms, their goals, objectives and motives. It is said that 'social organizations would vary in purpose, in constitution, in the methods and technologies through which they used to achieve their purpose. Further, they exist in different economic political and social environments and in different cultures and sub culture' (Wool house 1988).

Social organizations may have vision, mission and plan of action, which may be well articulated but sometimes it can be vague too. Social organizations need competent and skilled human resources. Those who govern are called owners, the custodians, the trustees ; those who manage are termed as management and those who operationalize the mission of the organizations are called functionaries or sometimes addressed as workforce. Those who are benefited out of the programs of the social organization are called beneficiaries sometimes they are addressed as clients, cases etc. Social organizations not only need human resources and structures but also need infrastructure and other resources such as land, building, machines, materials, and money etc. but the supreme significance has to be attached to the knowledge, skills, attitude, value and work and many such aspects of human resources engaged in the social organizations. The collection of research literatures are from international and national books, journals, websites ,published and unpublished research studies are presented orderly in year wise.

Adam (1963) gives equity theory, which examines relationships in terms of inputs and outcome. The basic premise is that outcome can be maximized equitably. In relation of consumer behavior they are said to compare the cost (inputs) of the product to the benefits received (outputs)

Swan (1977): If the comparison is equitable, satisfaction occurs then the research in the consumer area has indicated that satisfaction is related to fulfillment of expectance.

Verghese(1977; 1979) hailed voluntary action groups as new missionaries. Many of these have made important contributions to the well-being of a select group of neglected local people and the general public. Another contribution has been in the formation of a counter force or a credible critique mechanism of government policies

Charyulu in his study (1981: 219), while explaining the concept and importance of voluntary organizations, states: "A distinction is drawn by some writers between non-official organizations and voluntary organizations. To them, all non-official organizations are not necessarily voluntary. The test for voluntariness is that the organization has to try and stimulate voluntary action in the served community. It has to incorporate progressively to the enlightened individuals belonging to the community served in the higher echelons of its decision-making machinery. Another distinguishing point made out between these bodies is that voluntary organizations are spontaneous in their origin whereas the non-official agencies may be sponsored by the state"

Harris (1982) who explained the need for rural development, they state that as a policy and process approach, rural development is broader than 'agricultural development' and should take care of the development of the economy of the rural people and should lay particular focus on poverty and inequality in the rural society. It has an implied concern with reduction of inequalities in income, employment, access to public goods and services and with the alleviation of poverty.

Kabra (1985), further observes that "voluntary efforts have to be at best catalytic agents to energise the backward sections dominant articulation and mobilization potential for development. Voluntary action does not have to move totally along lines parallel to plan programmes; but it must not merge with them or become dependent on them. As a watchdog and corrective, it has to build an alternative fact of power so that politics of planning changes in favour of the poor".

Singh and Singh (1985: 24) elaborately discusses the concept of rural development. They consider rural development as a scheme of development for rural (non-urban) areas and therefore implies a special focus on irrigation facilities, electricity and the techniques of cultivation and the like, in these areas. In a narrow sense, in rural development, agriculture is not only the heart but almost the whole or rural development (ibid.:25).

Singh and Singh (1985: 138-139) classified the voluntary agencies as per their approaches in dealing with various kinds of problems of the people and the areas, as given below:

1. Charity: Giving food, clothing, medicine, alms in cash and kind, land, buildings etc.

2. Welfare: Providing facilities for education, health, drinking water, roads, communication etc.

3. Relief: Responding to call of duties during natural calamities like floods, droughts, earthquakes and man-made calamities like refugee influx, ravages of wars etc.

4. Rehabilitation: Continuing and follow-up of the work in areas struck by calamities and starting activities durable in nature.

5. Services: Building up infrastructure in depressed and backward areas, like tractor hiring services, providing or facilitating credit, supply of seeds, fertilizers, informing technical know-how,etc.

6. Development of socio-economic environment and all-round human beings: Socio-economic transformation on the area basis, covering all the people in a given area or concentrating only on a particular group normally neglected and in need of help.

7. Development of human beings: Conscience-raising, awakening, conscientising, organizing, recording of priorities to suit social justice, redeeming the past and opening doors to opportunities to the oppressed and exploited.

Rappaport (1987); Zimmerman and Rappaport (1988): Empowerment is the ability of individuals to gain control socially, politically, economically and psychologically through: (1) access to information, knowledge and skills; (2) decision making; and

and (3) individual self-efficacy, community participation, and perceived control. In the long term, the aim of NGOs is to promote sustainable community development through activities that promote capacity building and self reliance.

Vasant Desai (1988: 47) in his Rural Development: Experiments in Rural Development (Vol.IV) highlights the problems of the rural community and explains the approach of voluntary organizations in rural development. He states that "the problems of the rural community are not so simple as to be solved easily. Over the years, their problems have been aggravated and there is a feeling among the downtrodden that everybody who approaches them has a selfish and exploitative motive. Therefore, the task of the implementing agency is to regenerate confidence in the people about its selfless and dedicated approach to their problems. To solve their problems, a fair degree of technical and managerial competence is essential in a variety of fields, like agriculture, irrigation, plant protection, storage, marketing, education, animal husbandry, cottage industries, health and sanitation. Further, social service areas like health and education also require innovative approaches, beyond just opening a dispensary or construction of a school building. For this, voluntary agencies should develop "professionalism with the human touch".

Pradip N.Khandwalla (1988: 28) referring to Parsons (1956) states that "the potential of voluntary organizations to contribute to socio-economic development of poor, underdeveloped societies may vary markedly. To survive, organizations must meet one social need or another".

(Pandey,1991). Many such groups have demonstrated immense organizational and managerial efficiency in empowering people. Several of them have envisioned innovative ways of organizing people according to their cultural aspirations and indigenous goals. By experimenting and acting against the existing systems and development paradigms, some groups have increasingly stressed human development and structural transformation. They represent a new force in the developmental policies of the developing countries. By working as effective pressure groups they publicise the perceptions of people's front and bring pressure to bear upon authorities to make adequate provisions for poor people's felt-needs.

Masterson (1991) services provide an opportunity for an interface experience, which occurs between the client and the service organization during service delivery. The experience involves a total transaction between the client (on emotional, cognitive, and physical levels) and the service provider (through personnel, physical facility, and technology).

Harkness and Hensley (1991) demonstrated that clients of workers who received client-focused supervision were much more satisfied with the services they received than clients of workers who received traditional supervision. Client outcomes can facilitaties identifying client outcome measures.

Rapp and Poertner (1992) provide a useful typology identifying client outcomes and measures. This typology identifies client outcomes as Changes in effect,Changes in knowledge,Changes in behavior,Changes in environment, Changes in status.

A quality focus, however, must go beyond acknowledging quality as an organizational goal. It requires the analysis of customer satisfaction and the use of measurement tools to specifically address quality issues. Quality guru W.Edward Deming has often been quoted as saying, "If it isn't measured. It won't happen."

Holmberg and Sandbrook (1992) the Rio Conference interpreted sustainable development as a single process with three dimensions. In addition, the Johannesburg Plan of Implementation defined it as three distinct processes of "economic development, social development and environmental protection – as interdependent and mutually reinforcing pillars" (United Nations 2002). These dimensions were originally introduced with the aim of identifying areas in which social, economic and environmental goals are interrelated. However, these dimensions of sustainable development have done little to reduce the complexity of the concept and has itself introduced a contradiction

Lucy (1993:421), in her "Social Reforms to Voluntarism in India", traced the history of voluntarism. According to her, "voluntary action, synonymous with community action is as old as community or civilization itself. Voluntary action is a part and parcel of Indian Society". Further, while quoting Paul Chawdhary, she explains the difference between voluntary action and non-official organization: "Vinobhaji equates voluntary action with the concept of 'Janasakthi'. So long as the activity is undertaken by an agency, organization or institution which is native to the people concerned and which works without interference or dictation from outside, it should be regarded as voluntary action:". She further observes that "the test for voluntaries is that the organization has to try and stimulate voluntary action in the served community. It has to also progressively in corporate enlightened individuals belonging to the community to serve in the higher echelons of its decision-making machinery. Another distinguishing point is that the voluntary organizations are spontaneous in their origin where as the non-official agencies may be sponsored by the state".

Dhanagare (1993), states that "the NGOs are variedly known as 'voluntary action', welfare groups, etc., supposedly these groups have emerged to educate conscientise and mobilize the marginalized groups and the oppressed poor. The action groups function at the micro level, and associate themselves with the weaker sections to bring about social transformation".

Mehta (1994: 1) points out that development has to provide increasing opportunities to all the people for better living. It has to bring about more equitable income and wealth distribution to promote social justice and efficiency of production, provide a variety of facilities like education, health services, nutrition, housing, etc Mehta (op.cit.:48-49) states that voluntary organizations are not homogeneous in nature. There are various categories of voluntary organizations, depending on their aims and objectives. They are broadly categorized as "socio-economic, socio-cultural, rural development societies, cultural organizations and service-oriented organizations and societies". Mehta (op.cit.: 49), while explaining the various stages of voluntary action, points out that "in a developing country, voluntary action has a three-stage process. First, it is based on social conscience which has been defined by Beveridge in his work Voluntary Action, as "the feeling of discomfort on the part of people in comfort about the people in discomfort". Second, voluntary action has emerged from social consciousness generated by organized interest groups of people who are committed to people-centred approach. Third, organizations of various target groups, particularly from among the weaker sections, have emerged. The membership of these groups of associations generally cuts across traditional boundaries of caste and occupational groups. Voluntarism in India is going through a process of evaluation from altruism for its own sake, to conscientious activity dictated by the needs of the situation, i.e., requirement of the area and the people. So, the voluntary agencies choose a particular area for a particular task of development or welfare of the societies".

Sisir Basu (1994:8), in his article "Rural Poor: Failure of Growth Models", highlighted the plight of the rural poor, loopholes of planned development, policies and programmes and the necessity of organizing the poor. Stating that the need for organizing the poor is debated without any intensive analysis conceptually or operationally, Basu underscores the skepticism and vagueness that surround this concept. He opines that for the success of redistributive laws, policies and programmes, the poor should be organized and made aware of the benefits intended for them.

Sharma (1996: 28-39) states that "philanthropy is not charity, or doing out money to the distressed and the poor (...). It is a universally acknowledged fact that philanthropy is a creative work which puts a check on the degeneration of the persisting institutional mechanism with a view to reconstruct a better and the desired type of society. Religious revivalism, health and hospitals, literacy and education, civic and public amenities, social services for the distressed people, etc., are the most known activities undertaken by the voluntary action groups all over the world".

Rajesh Tandon (1996:1) in his work Changing Context and Challenges for Voluntary Action in India Today discusses the recent controversy in regard to CAPART 'blacklisting' 500 voluntary organizations for misuse of funds. This has resulted in a debate centering around the authenticity and accountability of voluntary action.

Rakesh Kapoor (1996: 13-14) while writing on "Voluntary Action: Survival, Politics and Transformation" broadly identify the various areas of voluntary sector such as "registered organizations and unregistered groups, grassroots organizations and urban support groups, networking organizations, development groups and welfare groups, a political organizations and politically active formations, non-profit organizations and not-for-profit organizations".

Soorya Moorthy (1997: 63-70), while highlighting the importance of NGOs in the development process of the Indian society, maintains that pre-independence NGOs limited their role to charity, relief and welfare activities. The complexion of NGOs changed in the late seventies. Presently, they are operating in almost all areas of human activity. However, there are also some limitations which are mostly common to the NGOs. There is a lot of criticism against the NGOs in relation to their sincerity and faith in service, corruption and organization etc.

Bridger (1997) has mentioned, sustainable community development includes five dimensions. The first dimension emphasizes on increasing local economic diversity. The second is self reliance which entails the development of local markets, local production, local processing of previously imported goods, and greater cooperation among local economic entities. The third dimension involves a reduction in the use of energy, coupled with the careful management and recycling of waste products. The fourth dimension focuses on the protection and enhancement of biological diversity and careful stewardship of natural resources. Finally, the fifth dimension is related to the commitment of the sustainable communities to social justice. Through the functions of providing microfinance, initiating capacity building and self reliance, NGOs could promote empowerment among community members, and eventually community sustainable development.

Streeten (1997) NGOs are professionally staffed organizations aiming at contributing to the reduction of human suffering and to the development of poor countries.

Lakshmaiah (1999,45) in his Tribal Development: The Role of Voluntary Organizations states that "the need of voluntarism was felt inevitable even in the first five-year plan. It was with this reason, the Government of India had made a provision to voluntary organizations to work in tribal areas as the people from voluntary organizations can stimulate the interest in the community with their innovative attitude, with their pragmatic approach, it is easy for them to break the ice and make inroads into their problem situations. They are at ease to inculcate leadership qualities among the tribal by building up awareness and instilling conscientisation measures. The basic philosophy behind voluntary effort is to make the people aware and lead them to the goal of self-reliance. Since the government programmes are time-bound and target oriented, the government functionaries are unable to make adequate rapport with the tribal people in the process of their interaction".

Srivastava (1999:13) while referring to Verghese (1977; 1979) and Pandey (1991) focused on "The Better Side of Voluntary Action". He stated that "the strident criticism of voluntary action groups in India does not, however, undermine the value of voluntary action in the current development phase. It is true that what the critics are condemning is not voluntary action as such, but only certain kinds of voluntary work done by certain people. The general consensus borders round the fact that the growth of NGOs signifies the search for alternative development paradigms with emphasis on popular mobilization or to supplement the state endeavours in several critical development sectors. The Government also recognizes the fact that voluntary organizations perform the function of fillings up the gaps in the statutory welfare services for people in need.

(Lawani, 1999: 17) "Generally, voluntary agencies and non-official organizations are treated as one and the same. This may not be so. All non-official organizations are not necessarily voluntary. Voluntary organizations are spontaneous in their origin whereas non-official agencies may also be government-sponsored"

Katar Singh (1999: 288), while highlighting the importance of NGOs in rural development, states that rural development should be considered as a joint effort of the people, corporate, cooperative and private sectors, for which a systems approach has to be adopted for an all-round and balanced development of the economy. In this effort as he points out NGOs have a special role in educating and training rural people and in ensuring their participation in rural development programmes, by working along with them (ibid.:289).

Sudha and Bhargava (2000: 21), while writing on the role of "Panchayats and NGOs in Social Change" states that "the role of voluntary organization is seen as complementary and supplementary to that of the government, as because they can act as watchdog to see that the development programmes are implemented properly. Without people's voluntary participation, no development programme can be a success. Panchayati Raj Institution (PRIs) have, therefore, to provide opportunities for the NGOs to involve in the task of making democracy and its fruits available to the people. These agencies must foster growth of grassroots leadership operating within the frame work of the state". Public participation can be encouraged by combined efforts of voluntary agencies and the government. Both are the main institutions of rural development and can lead to democratic decentralization by enabling the citizens to acquire self-confidence, self-reliance and participation (ibid.:23).

Bradshaw and Winn (2000) have noted, sustainability is rooted largely in an environmental approach, particularly in the industrialized countries. But, the goal of sustainable development is to find a balance between three pillars social, economic and environmental of communities

Gopal Krishna Shahu (2000:20-21) while discussing the "Role of Voluntary Organizations in Rural Development"observed that "during the 1980s the country witnessed tremendous proliferation and growth of voluntary issues. Since then, in the eradication of poverty illiteracy, ill-health and overall backwardness of the villagers, voluntary organizations played a commendable role. They were instrumental in initiating, stimulating and accelerating the process of change in the trading-bound rural societies. They also created awareness among the people about the developmental programmes."

Christopher (2000) conducted a study on the role of the NGO's in behaviour change communication in sexual health interventions in India-an evaluation study. This study was based on an evaluation study undertaken by the author to assess the role of the NGOs in behaviour change communication in HIV/AIDS prevention programmes in rural and urban areas in Madurai city and its surrounding villages. The questions that are raised were: How do these NGOs design BCC interventions and strategies? How was the programme implemented? What were the indicators followed for measuring the services outcomes? The study used both qualitative data and survey questionnaire for eliciting information from a representative sample of project administrators and Service personnel of NGOs. The data was analysed using elements of quantitative and qualitative research approaches. It was reported that NGOs in India have been making significant contributions in the HIV/AIDS prevention programmes. They adopt various intervention strategies to work with different target audiences who are considered "high risk groups". Many NGOs had realised the need for using behaviour change communication as a prevention strategy.

Nityananda (2000; 36-43), in his study; The Emerging Role of NGOs in Rural Development of India, discussed the challenges of development, evolution of NGOs in India, state-NGO relationship in India, new development paradigm and increasing role of NGOs and challenges and concerns for NGOs. As he points out, the term 'NGO' is quite loose and ambiguous. The role of NGOs is increasingly considered as vehicles for development. Conceptually, the term 'NGO' refers to a wide variety of non-profit organizations including religio-political institutions, welfare wings of religious organizations, business associations, cultural or scientific associations, associations for promotion of sports and arts, etc. (ibid.:36-37).

Thakur (2000) conducted a survey in Nepal to identify the capacity building needs of the local NGOs. The survey found out that local NGOs need training mainly on three areas i.e.1) Mobilization of people's cooperation and local resources, 2) Project planning, writing and implementation including account keeping and audit and (3) Preparation of technical resource materials like local curriculum, learning materials training of instructors and supervisors and learners achievement tests. After the survey the NRC-NFE, Nepal developed manual for training of the NGO personnel. Therefore there must be serious attempt to provide appropriate training opportunities to NGO personnel in different fields to build their capacities. There were several suggestions given by the author for proper functioning of the NGO's as to encourage the local people to set up their own NGOs called Community Based Organizations (CBOs). At present NGOs workers learn from trial and error method on the job. This is not very satisfactory situation. Similarly NGOs are said to be donor dependent. The fact is that the NGOs in the developing countries do not have their own source of income and the governments in many countries do not give any financial help to NGOs. So they have to seek help from NGOs or other donors. What is required is that the governments in the developing countries should have clear policy how the government and NGOs could work together. There could not be situation where only government could do all the jobs. Similarly the NGOs also cannot do all the tasks without government's help. This is the age of democracy whereby the civil society should be made strong. It is already very clear to the governments and donors that, the government should not and cannot do everything. The government and NGOs should work together helping and complementing each other.

Bradshaw and Winn (2000) have noted, sustainability is rooted largely in an environmental approach, particularly in the industrialized countries. But, the goal of sustainable development is to find a balance between three pillars social, economic and environmental of communities

Andre Beteille (2001: 298-299) in his "Civil Society and the Good Society" states that "the interest in voluntary action, voluntary movements and voluntary associations has been given a new lease of life by the concern for the creation or revival of civil society, particularly in the countries of Asia, Africa and Latin America. It has acquired a global dimension. A democratic society cannot function properly, not to speak at its growing, if everything in it is left to the state or even to statutory bodies. Mere statutory action will be infructuous if it is not underpinned by voluntary action. The significance of voluntary action and voluntary associations in the life of a democratic society has been brought to light by many".

Baviskar (2001: 5), while highlighting the importance of 'NGOs and Civil Society", in India, refers to Fisher (1997) and states that "the NGO sector in India is characterized by tremendous diversity and heterogeneity. Ignoring this diversity, unfounded generalizations are often put forward and unfair comments and criticisms are offered. NGOs differ from one another in size, in funding, in functions, in the levels at which they operate, and in organizational structures, goals and membership

Jagannathan (2001) studied the role of nongovernmental in Primary education a study of six NGO's in India. In this study of six NGOs working with school-age children in India, the researcher reported the potential benefits of a government-NGO alliance to achieve universal primary education. The author emphasized several areas in which collaboration can be particularly fruitful like, 1) Targeting under-served children: The Government could support the efforts of NGOs to bring out-of-school children into schools, through timely supply of teachers, classroom space, and other resources. Targeted action was needed to reach different types of out-of-school children - those who work, those who live in slums, those on the street, those who were members of tribes, or of migrant families, and those who live in places without schools. To encourage young, first-generation learners to stay in school requires a supportive and nurturing environment. To help make learning interesting and worthwhile for such children, teachers in government schools could receive special training in new methods developed by NGOs. 2) Enhancing quality: Improving the quality of education requires working closely with key agents of change, such as teachers, school heads, school management committees, and village education committees. To develop a cadre of trainers for primary school teachers, teacher training institutes would do well to evaluate, and learn from NGO models for teacher training. Teachers need a range of knowledge, and skills to teach underprivileged children effectively. Here again, NGO models would be a useful tool for teacher training institutes. NGOs and the government could collaborate in developing appropriate, and flexible learning assessment tools, in line with innovative teaching, and learning methods. But without safeguards, large-scale replication by the government of such NGO innovations as the "alternative school" and the "voluntary teacher" could lower the quality of education. 3) Government-NGO links: The Government and NGOs will need to share a common vision on how to achieve universal primary education if India is to reach this goal. NGOs can be credible partners with the government in shaping policies for primary education. This entails collaboration, rather than parallel initiatives by NGOs. To stay at the cutting edge in education, NGOs should continually evaluate, and refine their models. If NGOs are to play a policy role in education, two areas that have been neglected will need to be addressed - NGO capacity building, and organizational development. The survey has highlighted the need for specially designed strategies and initiatives for children that were still out of school. The NGOs surveyed and demonstrated that specific initiatives to address particular target groups, were required e.g., working children, street children, slum children, children of migrant families and tribal children. In order to accelerate the move towards UEE, it was suggested to be necessary for the Government to take a strong stance on elementary education as a "child right". Designing appropriate access strategies was contingent upon the availability of data on the number and character of the unreached. Governmental and non-Governmental estimates vary, for instance on the number of child labourers, where non-Governmental estimates are more than double of the Government. For the urban uneducated, there was a problem of estimation of numbers as Government data collection does not extend to unrecognized colonies. Similarly, remote and school-less habitations and hamlets did not get covered in Government surveys. It was important to use the NGOs and other independent bodies to develop reliable estimates of the out of school children. The Government relies on NGOs to provide schooling to the 'hardest to reach'. However, as NGO mobilization brings an inflow of children into schools, the Government should back up their efforts by providing timely classroom space and teachers.

Baccaro (2001) shows how particular NGOs can promote the organization and "empowerment" of the poor, particularly poor women, through a combination of micro-credit, awareness raising, training for group members, and other social services.

Baccaro (2001) They do this in various ways, e.g. by funding projects, engaging in service provision and capacity building, contributing to awareness, and promoting the self-organization of various groups.

Stromquist (2002) has noted three major functions for NGOs such as (1) service delivery (e.g. relief, welfare, basic skills); (2) educational provision (e.g. basic skills and often critical analysis of social environments); and (3) public policy advocacy.

Langran (2002), has mentioned that NGOs through capacity building help to sustain community development. NGOs are often created in order to expand the capacities of people (Korten 1990). Furthermore, NGOs are praised for promoting community-self-reliance and empowerment through supporting community based groups and relying on participatory processes (Korten 1990; Clark 1991; Friedmann 1992; Fowler 1993; Edwards and Hulme 1994; Salamon 1994). On the other hand, sustainable development has emerged over the past few decades as an important paradigm for community development

Rajkumar (2002: 64) while explaining the role and importance of NGOs in capacity building of panchayats for rural development states that "a plethora of development programmes run by government could not reach out to the poor due to various reasons. A closer examination of the views expressed by think-tanks in this regard reveals that adoption of alien development paradigm, incompatible with the social-cultural ethos, ossified bureaucratic set-up, corruption and pilferage, are some of the commonly discussed factors inhibiting developmental initiatives. Many factors are responsible for this change in perspective. These include persistent failure of the political and permanent executives in taking policy benefits to the citizens, leading to erosion of their confidence, changing perceptions of the United Nations and other specialized international agencies towards development with a human face and worldwide recognition of NGOs for championing the cause of people's empowerment, environment and sustainable social development".

Satish Deshpande (2003: 263), while discussing the plight of "Indian Social Science in the Contemporary Era" highlights the importance of non-governmental organizations. He states that "non-governmental organizations (NGOs) have proliferated and are now important sources of funding and demand for research; they are also fast emerging as preferred employers for young researchers".

Puri (2003) conducted a study on evaluation of the role of NGO's in the tribal development in India and it was found that out of seven NGOs, the nature of work of three NGOs was purely constructive. Nature of one NGO's work was purely agitational whereas three NGOs work was both - constructive and agitational. Almost all NGOs had said that their target group was mainly tribals in the Raigad district. Some of them, along with the tribal, also work for the women, oppressed people (dalit), small farmers, labourers and children. It was further found that some NGOs had shifted their focus from tribal to the other sections, in search of new project funding which was linked to the 'survival of the NGOs'. Many a times, the new target group was chosen only because that was the priority area of the funding organisation.

Saha and Chan (2003) conducted a study on NGOs in India : A Cross-Sectional Study. It was found that the NGOs in India had no reticence and their private status permitted them to operate without state control; they are free from political considerations. Thus about one thousand NGOs, including socio-cultural organizations, such as arts clubs, total literacy program, and cultural promotion groups, in the southern state of Kerala were successful in achieving economic and social development goals to enrich the quality of life, and the state government appreciated their efforts by offering funds. At the same time there appeared to be conscious attempts by many NGOs there not to fall prey "to the distortion of mission". Likewise, the governmental support to the SEWA, the most celebrated women's private empowerment organization in India, "could successfully lobby the government in favour of women in the informal sector," testifies to the authors' claim that cooperative and friendly relations could be built between the government and the NGOs, provided the organizations accepted good "strategy and programs."

Rajesh Tandon (2004, Jan 20,The Hindu) in his "Policy on Voluntary Sector", while referring to Planning Commission's policy document, clearly highlights how the government is giving importance to the role of voluntary sector and that, "as if they were primarily charitable, service delivery, welfare-oriented, relief and rehabilitation type of voluntary organizations which primarily work at the grassroots level to alleviate sufferings of the poor and the marginalized; to respond to failure in government services by filling gaps in social services delivery and in the welfare of the weaker sections".

Hibbard and Tang (2004), in their study in Vietnam, have noted the importance of NGOs' roles in sustainable community development. One of the roles was that NGOs balance the social, economic and environmental factors in promoting sustainable development. Another important role of NGO that they discovered was decentralization of the central government which helps the local communities to acquire more power in order to make their own decisions. But, sometimes the local communities lack specialists to do professional work and resources that are important for the particular projects. In this situation, NGO assists local staff with drafting sustainable development plans that are functional under the umbrella of a central government policy. Finally, they concluded that sustainable community development is process oriented, and it requires extensive community participation and relies on network to share resources, knowledge and expertise. From the literatures, it could be summarized that NGOs play an important function in promoting sustainable community development. Sustainable community development emphasizes on a balance between environmental concerns and development objectives, while simultaneously enhancing local social relationships. Sustainable communities meet the economic needs of their residents, enhance and protect the environment, and promote more humane local societies.

Desai (2005) has mentioned that NGOs have an important role to play in supporting women, men and households, and expected that they can meet the welfare. She accounted some role and functions for NGOs, such as counseling and support service, awareness raising and advocacy, legal aid and microfinance. These services help the people to achieve their ability, skill and knowledge, and take control over their own lives and finally become empowered

Gupta *et. al.* (2007) conducted a study on the Introduction of New Health Technologies in India: Role of civil society and NGOs. In addition to the private commercial sector, civil society and NGOs often play critical roles in the introduction of new health technologies. NGOs were frequently responsible for providing on-the-ground services, especially in remote areas where government programmes may not reach. A vibrant NGO sector had demonstrated its capacity to reach many marginalized groups and to appropriately address sensitive health and social issues. All of these could contribute to the successful adoption, implementation, and uptake of an AIDS vaccine in India. This study was taken up to assess key issues in the introduction of health technologies in India, with the aim of anticipating challenges that may one day face AIDS vaccines. The researcher highlighted some of the lessons learned that can help India prepare for a successful experience with AIDS vaccines and discussed the challenge of introducing new technologies in India and the particular challenge of AIDS vaccines. It was found that countries that do not face a generalised epidemic, including India, will most likely target the vaccines to specific populations. The target groups, including possibly sex workers, migrant workers, injecting drug users, and men who have sex with men, are difficult to reach, often due to legal issues and social mores. While there are health and social services that reach such target groups, especially those provided by NGOs, difficulties in identifying and reaching those individuals will undoubtedly affect potential coverage levels for AIDS vaccines. There may also be additional challenges in securing political support and financial commitments for programs targeted only to certain groups. Finally, and related to the point above, delivery of AIDS vaccines to adolescents and adults would likely take place outside the traditional childhood immunisation programme. Despite any shortcomings childhood immunisation programmes may have, they do have an established infrastructure and a ready means of reaching their target population. AIDS vaccines, however, will likely be targeted (at least initially) to adults and adolescents, and will therefore require new delivery and informational systems.

Prasad (2007) conducted a study on Jai Sri: Celebrating Civil Society involvement in SRI in India. This paper provided an overview of civil society engagement and spread of SRI in India. Examining why civil society contribution was important for SRI dissemination and adaptation in India, and what civil society organisations bring to the SRI agenda. The paper suggests that recognising this and understanding the changing dynamic of state civil society relation was critical for SRI uptake. Civil society involvement in SRI did not only enhanced the spread of SRI but also brought in important elements, like the establishment of criteria or axioms for research on SRI, and introducing dimensions of equity, gender and resource sustainability into the SRI debates. Using the broader idea of civil society to include not just NGOs or non-governmental organizations, but also formal and informal networks offarmers, the paper suggests that closer attention to the practices of civil society could help in scaling-up of SRI. There researcher gave recommendations for some mechanisms by which there could be a faster spread through a changed relation between civil society and other actors, from mistrust and encounters in the early history of SRI, to dialogues and learning alliances in the future. It was found that mechanisms for state agencies to use expert advice from NGOs and resource persons did not exist in sufficient measure, even though there was acknowledgement among the actors that this could enhance effectiveness. SRI did have the potential of addressing some of these challenges but it required a much higher level of collaboration between state, civil society and business organizations if a dent was needed to be made. NGOs and the state cannot see themselves as 'reluctant partners' and need to be seen as moving together in meeting some of the challenges. The history of civil society involvement suggests some possibilities where more effort could be made to convert reluctant partners to join learning alliances.

Singh (2008) studied on meeting the MDGs through the Human Right to Water – A gendered analysis in India from actor oriented perspective. It was found that one of the targets of the UN Millennium Development Goals (MDGs) is to halve the number of people without sustainable access to safe drinking water by 2015. This assumption has been examined by the authors within the scope of two different research projects supported by Sida-Sarec. Using an actor-oriented perspective that further made a distinction between 'implementation' and 'realization' of human rights, these projects attempt to understand how the globally formulated norms concerning water as a human right get translated into action at the local level. The first project looked at the HRW of women while the second one focuses on the right of children. The research was based upon empirical studies in different parts of India and refers to the right to water situation in areas affected by problems of water quality and quantity. The findings of the research indicate that realization of HRW essentially involves dynamics at the 'third level' of human rights implementation. This constitutes the interface between the community and the agency where action towards fulfillment of the right was ultimately unfolded. Following the rights-based approach to development, two kinds of actors were identified – the 'rights-holders' (women and children) and the 'duty-bearers' (government, NGOs, international development agencies). The contextual factors that influence the realization of the HRW of women and children as separate right-holder groups were classified into two categories: first, the nature of human rights approach adopted by the agency (if any) and second, the socio-cultural factors in the community context that lead to re-construction of the right at the local level. The dynamics of interaction between the two sets of factors are complex and need to be understood as contextual realities. On the whole, the latter have been found to have significant influence on the equitable, effective and sustainable realization of the HRW. From the preliminary findings of the research, it was concluded that mere legislative actions at international and national forums for implementing the HRW may not offer enough benefits towards ensuring progress towards the MDGs. There was a need to explore the dynamics at the 'third' level and consider how the learning could be integrated into the global and state initiatives so as to promote water justice for women and children.

2.3 Implications from the review of related literature

The several studies reviewed have revealed important findings and gaps in research in the area of NGO's and their social development contribution. Studies reviewed focus on the needs of NGO's, collaboration among different NGO's and among NGO's and government, role of NGO's in health, education, community development. One of the important aspect that has been reported is that the local NGOs need training mainly in areas like Mobilization of people's cooperation and local resources, project planning, writing and implementation including account keeping and audit, preparation of technical resource materials like local curriculum, learning materials training of instructors and supervisors and learners achievement tests. The implications drawn from the studies are stated below: Morales and Sheafor (1987) stated that "The skill of social work requires both the appropriate selection of techniques for a particular situation and the ability to use techniques effectively. Betty Baer and Ronald Federico (1978) have organized the skills component of practice into four areas : (i) Information gathering and assessment; (ii) The development and use of the professional self; (iii) Practice activities with individuals, groups and communities and (iv) Evaluations Werner W. Boeham, (1958) in his book "The nature of Social Work "suggests that professional skill is expressed in the activities of the social worker. It constitutes the social workers' artistic creation resulting from three internal processes : (i) Conscious selection of knowledge Pertinent to the professional task at hand, (ii) Fusion of knowledge with social work values and (iii) Expression of this synthesis in professional relevant activity. Professionally managed NGOs wouldlike to have type of personnel who possess skills and abilities in the areas of communication persuasion assertiveness skill in monitoring, designing, questioning, gathering data, giving and receiving of knowledge etc. which have direct bearing on interpersonal sensitivity. Further skills in counseling, interviewing, building rapport, probing, exploring, resolving conflict etc. are also of tremendous significance in the management of NGOs.

The review of literature helped to know more on the concept of development in various aspects of life. It has given insides on the efforts and contributions of NGOs for social development. The reviews reached the knowledge on the scope of NGOs at National and International level. Thus the researcher has presented review of literature which helped to form the interview schedule and to prepare research methodology for the study that is presented in Chapter-III.

Chapter - III

Research Methodology

3

Research Methodology

The term "methodology" in a literal sense means the science or study of methods (payne & payne, 2006). Thus social research methods are called methodological in approach. Methodology deals with the characteristics of methods, the principles on which methods operate, and the standards governing their selection and application. Methodology helps show how the research questions are constructed from prior orientations and knowledge. The methods chosen in the study are both quantitative and qualitative.

When total monetary and human resources involved in social organisations are huge, it is more pertinent to study social organisation from the point of view of their functionaries beneficiaries and infrastructure. Today we live in consumerist society in which consumer's satisfaction and delight are of tremendous value. The two consumers (one internal and one external) of NGO's are beneficiaries and functionaries. With these two human groups in the NGOs along with the type of infrastructure that they have, decide the presence and future of these NGOs. The beneficiaries of the social organisations are independent variable. It is because of them social organisations exist. Therefore it is essential to understand whether beneficiaries of the social organisations get effective, efficient and quality service or not.

In this chapter, researcher has presented a detailed description of the research methodology such as methods and procedures followed in the selection of the problem, sample, objectives, research context, development of research tools and techniques, data collection, data analysis and organisation of the study. Thus the present study is important to carryout, which has micro and marco level impact of NGOs and their functioning.

3.1 Statement of The Problem

The purpose of the present research is to study the contributions of NGOs for social development in the Vizianagaram District of Andhra Pradesh. The recent social inclusion policies of government of India highlighted the need for partnership for civil society for development and emphasised the contributions of Non-government organisations for grass root level interventions and rural transformation and development.

Social Organisations can be studied from various perspectives. They can be studied from the process point of view, constituent's point of view and evaluation, outcome or impact point, duplication of work and reach the un reached in a more meaningful way. The study will certainly help the policy makers and funding agencies to review and monitor the programs and nurture them in a strategic way and to work at bottom up level where the beneficiary out put is considered.

3.2 Objectives of The Study:

1. To study the profile, policies and programmes of social organisations(NGOs) in Vizianagaram district.
2. To study the activities of NGOs and their contributions for Development in various aspects ,
3. To study the socio-economic profile of the beneficiaries and their opinion on the self development of various aspects like social, economic, political, cultural and religious.

3.3 Research Context

The context of the present study is Vizianagaram district, one of the least developed districts in the state of Andhra

Pradesh. Vizianagaram district was formed on 1st June 1979, with headquarters at Vizianagaram as per G.O. Ms. No 700/ revenue (U) Department dated 15th May 1979 with portions carved from Srikakulam and Visakahapatnam Districts. Vizianagaram district extends over an area of 6,539 Sq.Kms with a density of 343 per Sq. KM covering 1,551 villages, out of which 66 are uninhabited. The total population of the district is 22,45, 103 as per 2001 census consisting of 11,20,124 Males and 11,24,979 females. According to 2001 census rural population of the district is 18.33 Lakhs which comes to 82% of the total population and the urban population is 4.12 Lakhs which comes to 18% of the total population.

The history of Vizianagaram district is connected with hoary past of Kalinga, one of the political divisions of ancient India. Only in modern times, the upper part of Kalinga was gradually merged into Orissa State and the lower part into Andhra Region. An important event in the history of the district is the war between the Rajas of Vizianagaram and Bobbili, popularly known as Bobbili Yuddham. The war was fought between the Rajah of Vizianagaram aided by the French General Bussy and the Rajah of Bobbili on the 24th of January 1757. The bravery and valour of the soldiers of Bobbili displayed in this war is still remembered by the people of the area.

Another important event in the history of the district is the war between the French and the English fought at Chandurthi in 1758 in which the French were defeated and the Northern Circars were made over to the British under a firmana from the Mughal Emperor, Shah Alam in 1765 which were placed under the then existing Chief and Council at Vizagapatam. In 1794, the Chiefs and Councils were abolished and Vizagapatam was arranged into three divisions each under a Collector. Almost the entire area of the present area of Vizianagaram district fell under the second division.

The history of the rebellions against the alien rule goes back to 1830s when the people of the district particularly the tribals, unable to beat the oppression, rose in frequent rebellions are leading to the establishment of separate administrative system known as "Agency Administration" under the India Act XXIV of 1839. The rebellion of Korra Malliah, a tribal chief of the Salur area against the British rule in 1900 is another important event in the struggle against the alien rule. The District Magistrate dispatched Reserve Police to suppress the revolt which was seriously resisted by the people. In the skirmish that followed many were killed. Korra Malliah along with his son was arrested and kept in Jail where he died subsequently. In the freedom struggle the people hailing from the area enthusiastically took part in various phases of the movement like a non-cooperation movement, civil disobedience movement, Quit India Movement etc.

After abolition of the Zamindaris in1948, Visakhapatnam district was found to be unwieldy for administrative purposes. Consequently, Srikakulam district was carved out in 1950, bifurcating it from Visakhapatnam district. The constitution of Vizianagaram district in 1979, by transferring the taluks of Parvathipuram, Kurupam, Salur, Bobbili, Badangi and Cheepurupalle from Srikakulam district and some taluks of Visakhapatnam forms the latest development in the history of the district 500 Years of glorious past and rich cultural heritage made Vizianagaram the cultural capital of Andhra Pradesh. It acquired a separate statehood in 1979. The Raja Saheb Dr. P.V.G. Raju who inherits the socialistic fervor and the spirit of religious tolerance from his ancestors, renounced his Zamindari with out taking any compensation and their fort is now entirely became the citadel of education which houses one of the oldest colleges (Maharaja College 1879) in India.

The social reformer , Sri Gurajada, the Poet singer Sri Adibhatla Narayana Das, the great wrestler Kodi Rma Murthy, the imaginative poet Sri Devulapalli Krishna Sastry were associated with the college in some form . The talented musicians Dwaram Vekata Swami Naidu, Saluri Rajeswara Rao and of late R.P. Pattanayak hail from this place. The divine singers Gantasala and Suseela who were the proud students of Maharaja College of Music added indescribable grace to the art of singing.

Table-3.1: Vizianagaram District Profile

Sr. No	*Name of Revenue Division*	*Name Of the Mandal*	*No of Revenue Villages*	*No of Panchayats*
1	Vizianagaram	Vizianagaram	23	21
		Gantyada	45	35
		Bhogapuram	22	22
		Denkada	28	26
		Pusapatirega	37	27
		S.Kota	40	26
		Jami	28	25
		Kothavalasa	28	25
		Vepada	39	29
		L.Kota	32	31
		Nellimarla	33	28
		Gurla	39	37
		Cheepurupalli	32	17
		Garividi	38	28

(Contd.)

(Contd. Table-3.1)

Sr. No	Name of Revenue Division	Name Of the Mandal	No of Revenue Villages	No of Panchayats
2	Parvathipuram	Merakamudidam	41	24
		Gajapathinagaram	35	28
		Bondapalli	33	26
		Dattirajeru	46	35
		Mentada	37	30
		Parvathipuram	54	26
		Komarada	99	31
		Garugubilli	34	28
		Jiyyammavalasa	58	31
		Kurupam	95	23
		Gummalaxmipuram	124	27

(Contd.)

(Contd. Table-3.1)

Sr. No	*Name of Revenue Division*	*Name Of the Mandal*	*No of Revenue Villages*	*No of Panchayats*
		Badangi	29	25
		Therlam	50	32
		Saluru	90	29
		Pachipenta	54	28
		Makkuva	54	21
		Ramabhadrapuram	32	22
		Bobbili	44	30
		Seethanagaram	44	34
		Balijipeta	34	24
Total			**1551**	**931**

(Source: Census Report, 2001, Government of India)

Besides its rich cultural heritage, the Vizianagaram district has the potential to attract the eyes of the tourists. Nestling between the Bay of Bengal and the eastern Ghats, the landscape of Vizianagaram with its captivating intensity would undoubtedly attract the overwhelming response of tourists. However, it is one of the developing districts in the state of Andhra Pradesh and therefore several developmental programs and projects have been in operation in the area by both government and non-government organisations.

The following table describes the profile of Vizianagaram district in terms of number of mandals, villages and panchayats.

Table-3.2: Population of Vizianagaram District

Population (in Lakhs)			
	Male	*Female*	*Total*
Population	11.19	11.30	22.49
S.C. Population	1.19	1.19	2.38
S.T. Population	1.06	1.09	2.15
Density of Population (Per Sq.Km.)			344

(Source: Census Report, 2001, Government of India)

Table-3.3: Demography and other Particulars of Vizianagaram District

Demography and Other Particulars	
Geographical Area (Sq. Kms)	6,539
Administration	
Revenue Divisions	2
Mandals	34
Villages	1551
No.of Habitations	3193
Towns	11
Municipalities	4
Gram Panchayats	931
Dairy Development	
No. of Milk Chilling Centres	2
Milk Collection Centres Coop. Societies	229
Pickup Centres	240
Average Monthly Procurement (lakh Ltrs.)	10.6

(Contd.)

(Contd. Table-3.3)

Industries	
No. of Large & Medium Scale Industries	22
No. of Registered Factories	509
No. of Small Scale Industries	3420
Rural Water Supply	
CPWS Schemes	6
PWS Schemes	432
Bore Wells	10454
Fisheries	
No. of Fishing villages	8
Coast line length (KMs)	28
Coastal Mandals	2
No. of Fishermen Families	1554
Roads (Length In Kms)	
National Highways	200
R & B	1757
P.R.	2722
Total	4679
Literacy Rate (percentage)	
Male	62.37
Female	39.91
Total	51.07
Bank Branches	
No. of Nationalised Banks	75
RRBS	56
Coop. Banks	17
Total	148
Post & Telegraphs	
No. of Post Offices	633
No. of telegraph Offices	50
Telephone Exchanges	77
Telephone connections	44975
Electricity	
Length of Transmission and Distributionlines (KMs)	16207
No. of villages electrified out of? 1585	1556
No. of service connections	353659
Power Consumption (MKHW)	?698
Connected load? (MKHW)	253
Land Holdings (2000-01 Census)	
Marginal Cultivators	307449
Small Cultivators	65767

(Contd.)

(Contd. Table-3.3)

Medium Cultivators	36970
Large Cultivators	779
Total	410965
Livestock Population (2004 Census In Lakhs)	
Cattle	4.00
Buffaloes	2.50
Sheep	5.13
Goats	1.97
Pigs	0.31
Poultry	21.30
Total Veterinary Institutions	138

(Source: Census Report, 2001, Government of India)

Map of Vizianagaram District

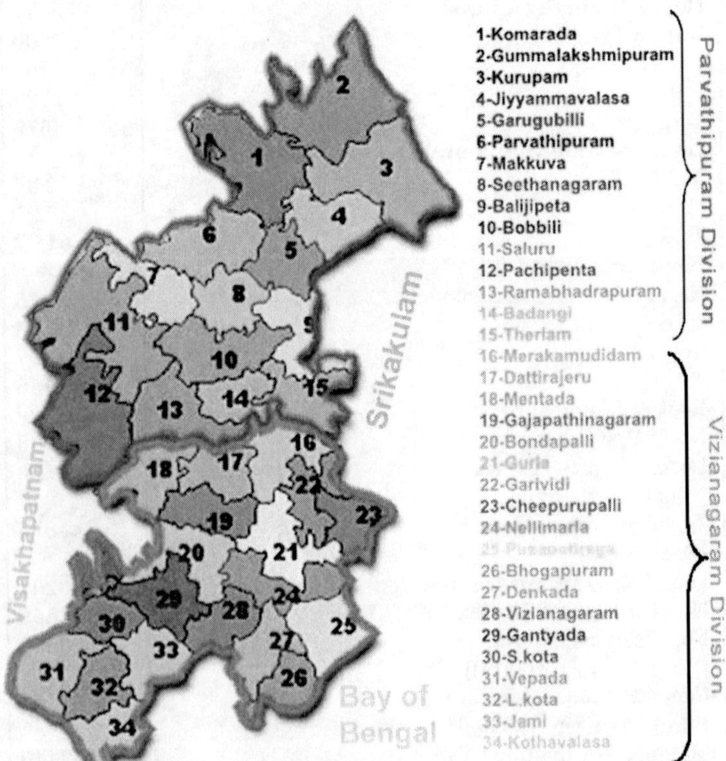

Table-3.4: Land Utilization in Vizianagaram District

Land Utilization (In Hect.)	*Area*	*% to G.A*
Total Geographical Area (G.A.)	630038	100.0
Forests	111977	17.8
Barren & Uncultivable Land	77753	12.3
Land put to non-agricultural uses	76172	12.1
Current Fallow Lands	24232	3.9
Others	31145	4.9
Net Area shown	308759	49.0

(Source: Census Report, 2001, Government of India)

3.4 Population

All the registered NGOs working in different revenue mandals of Vizianagram district constitute the population for the study. There are 34 revenue mandals in Vizianagaram district with 1551 villages. There are approximately 504 NGOs working in various mandals of Vizianagaram. They are working both in rural, tribal and urban areas focusing on various social development projects.

3.5 Sample For The Study

The researcher has approached the government offices like DRDA,IKP and the District NGOs forum and also consulted with well known experts and resource persons while preparing the final list of the NGOs for study.

A purposive sampling technique was used to select the sample for the study. The purpose for the inclusion of NGOs in sample is as follows;

- NGO should be a registered organisation under Society's Registration Act 1860, of Govt. of India.
- Should have at least 5 years of continuous field contribution in different mandals of Vizianagaram District.
- Should have an annual minimum funding of Rs. 5 lakhs and above for various social development programs.

The above criteria were followed to identify the potential NGOs, which are continuously extending their services for the social development. Thus a total of 99 NGOs were identified by the rese archer for conducting the present study.

The selection of the beneficiary for the study is taken on the basis of random sampling method. Ten beneficiaries from each NGO are considered, as the samle of 99NGOs and the total beneficiaries taken for the study are 990.

Table-3.5: Sample Distribution of NGOs

Sr. No	*Work context of NGO*	*Frequency N=99*	*Percentage (%)*
1.	Rural	53	53
2.	Urban	12	13
3.	Tribal	34	34
	Total	**99**	**100**

Table-3.6: Sample Distribution of Functionaries of NGOs

S. No.	*Designation of the Respondent*	*Frequency*	*Percentage (%)*
1.	Chief Coordinator	16	16
2.	Chief Secretary	25	25
3.	Project Director	10	10
4.	Project Manager	30	30
5.	Programme Coordinator	18	19
	Total	**99**	**100**

3.6 Delimitation Of The Study

The study is delimited to the NGOs working in various revenue mandals in Vizianagaram district not less than last five years with a minimum annual budget of Rs. Five lakhs.

3.7 Explanation Of The Term Used

The word "Contribution to social development" refers to the significant work of the NGOs for social development in terms of people's livelihood development. The word social development refers to all those factors contributing to the development of people and their life styles. This includes social ,economic, political ,cultural and religious aspects of developments as well as education, health, opportunities, capacity building, economy and freedom to choose and decision making etc.,

3.8 Tools And Techniques

Questionnaires for functionaries, Observation Schedules, Unstructured Interviews were used as the research tools to collect the relevant data. Researcher had constructed the questionnaire for the functionaries by focusing on the basic information of the organisation and their various programs for the social development. There are few open ended questions, where in the functionaries will respond to the questions pertaining to the issues and challenges they face and their strategic alliance with government.

Questionnaires for the beneficiaries and unstructured interviews were used as the research tool to understand the perceptions of the beneficiary towards their development in their various aspects of life.

Apart from the questionnaire, the researcher had conducted field studies, where the programs of the selected NGOs are taking place. These field visits were basically to observe the ground realities and to interact with the functionaries and beneficiaries to know their perceptions on the activities of the concerned NGO. Key personnel of the NGOs as well as the beneficiaries were identified and interviews were conducted to explore the contributions of NGOs.

a. **Document Analysis**: The researcher analysed the reports of the policies and programs of the NGOs for the purpose of the nature of policies pertaining to the social development

b. **Questionnaire** : Two separate questionnaires are framed for both functionaries and beneficiaries.It consists of both open ended and close ended Questions to understand the profile and programmes of the NGOs for development as well as beneficiaries development in various aspects of life.

c. **Participant observation**: The researcher personally visited the selected NGOs in Vizianagaram district to observe the ongoing programs to understand the actual transaction of the programs in terms of social development. This provided the researcher the first hand information about the actual implementation of various social development programs, perception of the functionaries and beneficiaries of the social development programs.

d. **Interviews**: The researcher conducted interviews with the various functionaries of the NGOs working in vizianagaram district to understand the functional difficulties and challenges of working with civil society for social development.

3.9 Data Collection

The Researcher personally visited all the selected NGOs with prior permission and administered the tools to collect the data. Interviews were conducted separately with the functionaries and beneficiaries of the selected NGOs. A detailed field notes was developed based on the recordings while interacting with the subjects of the study.

3.10 Data Processing And Analysis

The collected data has been classified, edited, coded. The coding of data is, the process of transferring the raw data into numerical values, which is used for the statistical purpose as well as tabulation .When the code book is finalized, the data will be turned into master chart then it processed into computer through MS EXCEL package.

The data was analysed qualitatively as well as quantitatively. The numerical data in terms of financial parameters, number of programs and the contributions were analysed with simple percentage. The qualitative data obtained from the interviews and observations were analysed qualitatively by describing the content of responses, portfolios developed through the field observations and the qualitative data of the interviews with functionaries and beneficiaries. The entire data analysis was presented in two sections where section one focuussed on Funtionaries of NGOs and section two for beneficiaries with respect to the objectives of the study.

3.11 Organisation Of The Study

The present study was conducted in a phased manner and presented in the thesis in five chapters as follows;

Chapter-I, deals with the overview on NGOs and introduction of the research problem from a broad perspective of social work and its importance for social development. A detailed elaboration on the term NGOs was presented to provide clarity on the nature and functions of NGOs in the social context.

The Chapter-II, highlights the detailed review of related literature in the area of Social development through Non-government organisations. This chapter also highlighted the implications of the research reviews for the present study.

In Chapter-III, research presented a detailed description of the methodology adopted for conducting the study. This includes the research context, population and sampling procedure, research tools used and scheme of data analysis.

Chapter-IV, provides a detailed analysis of the data with help of descriptive statistics and also qualitative descriptions. The analysis is presented as per the objectives of the study. The last chapter deals with the summary, suggestions and conclusions of the present study.

Chapter - IV

Data Analysis and Interpretations

4

Data Analysis and Interpretations

This chapter deals with analysis and interpretation of data gathered through research tools as stated in Chapter-3. The analysis is categorized and structured in two sections. The research study includes analysis and interpretation of the data about the nature and functions of the NGOs working in Vizianagaram district and focused on the analysis and interpretation of the data about the contributions of NGOs for the social development as viewed by them and opinions of the beneficiaries on their changes and development.

Section-1 Begins with the description of general socio-personal and work profile of the NGOs in Vizianagaram district. Section- 2 deals with the contributions of the NGO in terms of Social Economic, Political, Cultural and religious development as viewed by the beneficiaries and followed by detailed description of the data interpretations regarding the functional characteristics of the NGOs as viewed by beneficiaries.

The data procured through the Interviews with the functionaries and beneficiaries were also described. Finally, the concluding section highlights the analysis Of functionaries and beneficiaries in terms of contributions for development were done by NGOs and the views expressed on the changes taken place by beneficiaries are the parameters under the study.

The present study is focusing on the contributions of Non-Government Organizations in the Vizianagaram district of Andhra Pradesh and therefore the data was collected through the questionnaire, participant observation and the interviews with the functionaries and beneficiaries of the NGOs in terms of their composition, policies, programmes, nature of work and their impact on social development.

SECTION-I

The following Table 4.1.1 with graphical presentation clearly shows that the majority (30 per cent) of the respondents are the Project Managers of the NGOs whereas 10 per cent are project Directors and the remaining 25 per cent are Chief Secretaries, 19 per cent are Programme Coordinators, 16 per cent are Chief Coordinators. It is observed that key functionaries are mostly Project Managers and Chief Secretaries.

It is revealed from the following Table 4.1.2 and graphical presentation that the majority 75 per cent of the respondents have 0-3 years of work experience in the NGOs, whereas 9 per cent of respondents have got 6 and above years of experience the remaining 16 per cent have 4 to 5 years of experience.

The following Table 4.1.3 and graphical presentation narrates the facts that the various types of tasks assigned to the functionaries of the NGOs. The majority (34 per cent) of functionaries are assigned with income generating related issues. Whereas 7 per cent of functionaries are assigned with human rights. The remaining 26 per cent are assigned with health related tasks and 13 per cent for social issues, 12 per cent for environmental and 8 per cent for training and workshops.

The following Table 4.1.4 and graphical presentation shows that the majority (30 per cent) of the NGOs are established during the year 2001-2005. Whereas 22 per cent of NGOs are established during 1983-1988, the remaining 20 per cent are during 1989-1994 and 28 per cent are during 1995-2000.

The following Table 4.1.5 and graphical presentation shows that the majority (53 per cent) of NGOs are functioning with

Table-4.1.1 : Distribution of Functionaries of NGOs by Designation

S. No.	*Designation of the Respondent*	*Frequency*	*Percentage (%)*
1.	Chief Coordinator	16	16
2.	Chief Secretary	25	25
3.	Project Director	10	10
4.	Project Manager	30	30
5.	Programme Coordinator	18	19
	Total	**99**	**100**

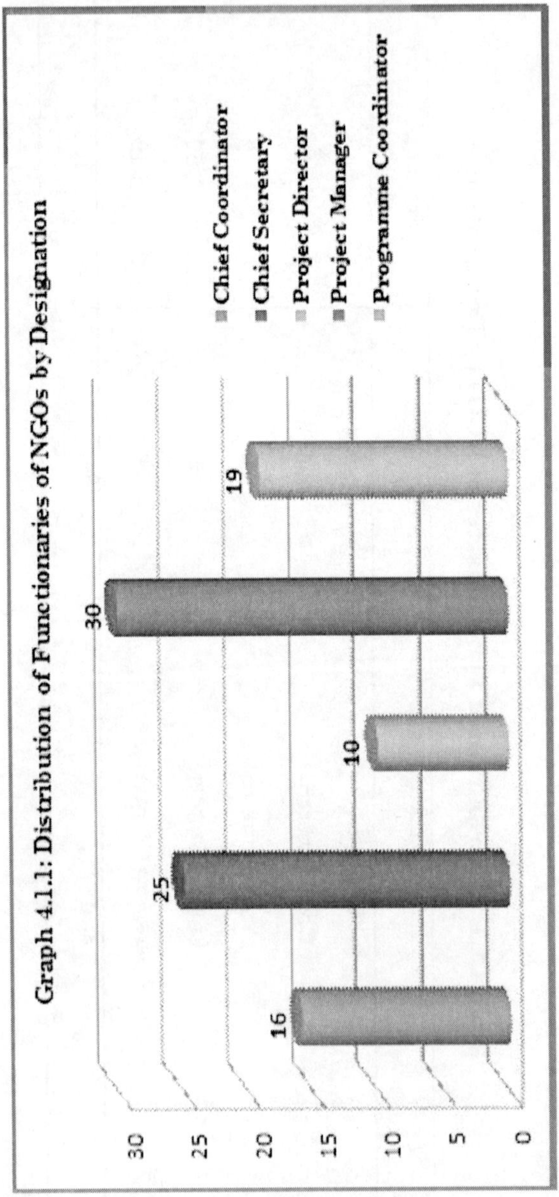

Graph 4.1.1: Distribution of Functionaries of NGOs by Designation

Table-4.1.2: Distribution of Functionaries by work experience

S. No	*Years of Experience*	*Frequency*	*Percentage (%)*
1.	0-3	75	75%
2.	4-5	15	16%
3	6 and above	09	09%
	Total	**99**	**100%**

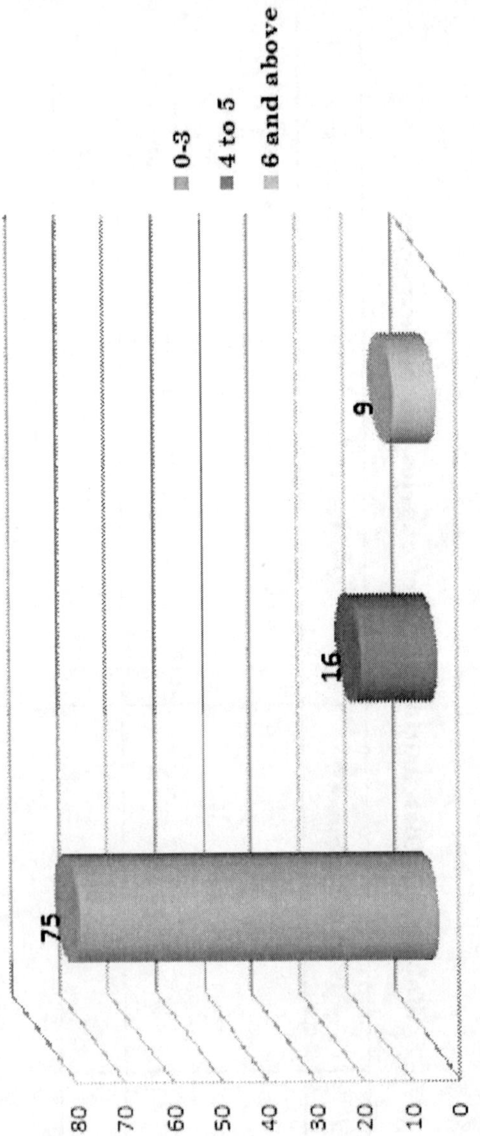

Graph 4.1.2: Distribution of Functionaries by work experience

Table-4.1.3: Distribution of Functionaries by Task Assigned

S. No.	*Nature of work assignment*	*Frequency*	*Percentage (%)*
1.	Income generation related	34%	34
2.	Social issues	13	13
3.	Environmental	12	12
4.	Training and Workshops	08	08
5.	Human rights	06	07
6.	Health related issues	26%	26
	Total	**99**	**100**

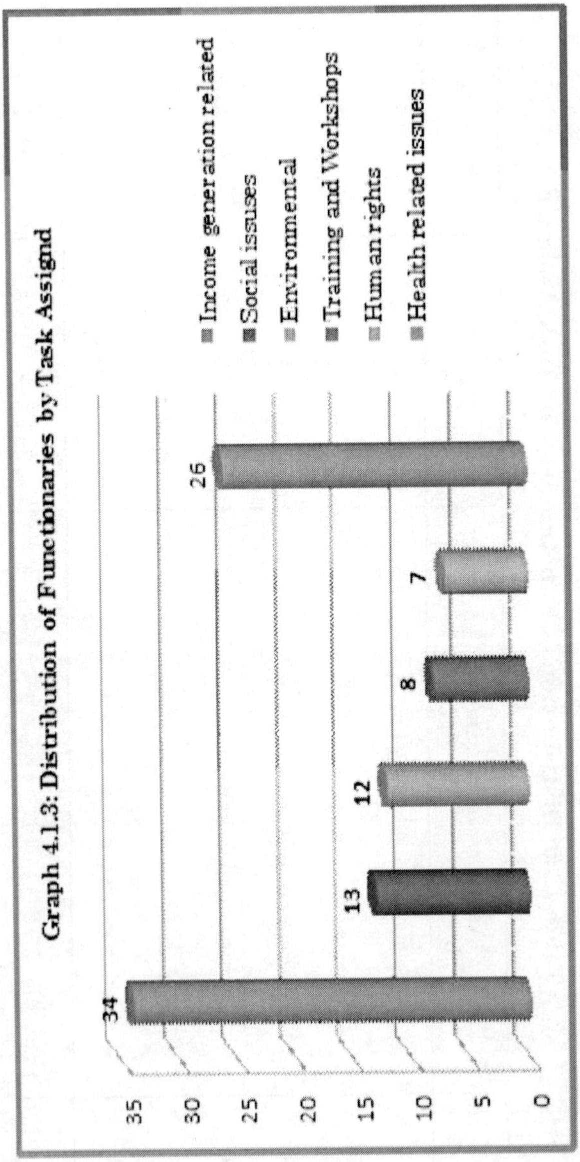

Graph 4.1.3: Distribution of Functionaries by Task Assignd

Table-4.1.4: Distribution of NGOs by Year of Establishment

S. No.	*Year of Establishment*	*Frequency*	*Percentage (%)*
1.	1983 – 1988	22	22
2.	1989-1994	20	20
3.	1995-2000	27	28
4.	2001-2005	30	30
	Total	**99**	**100**

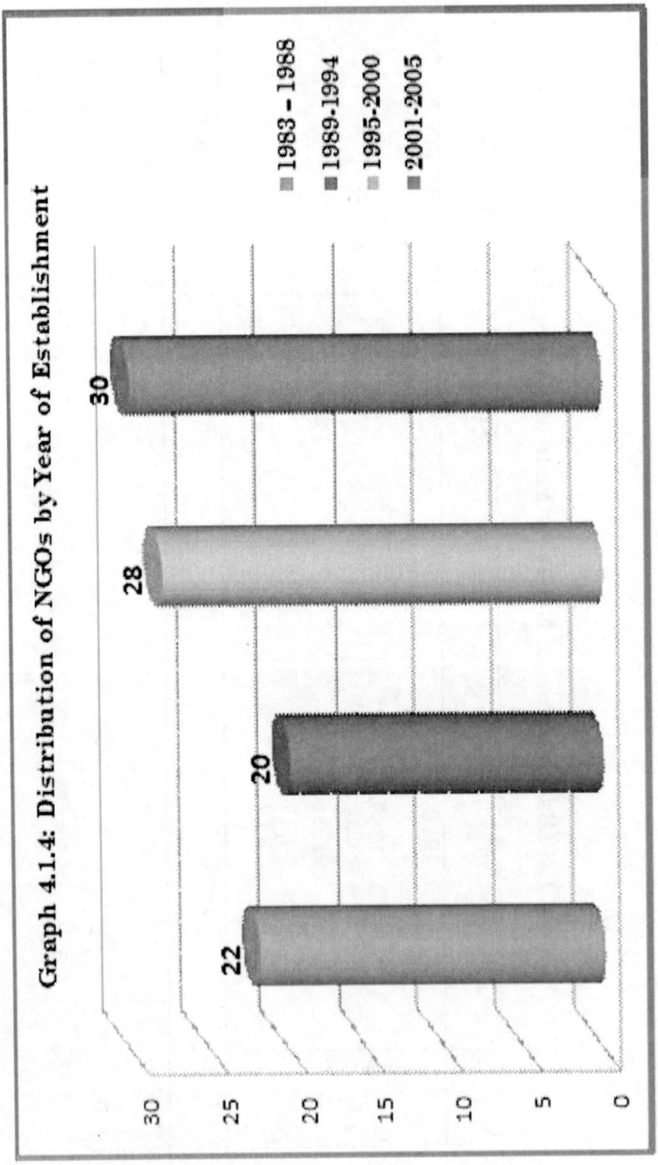

Graph 4.1.4: Distribution of NGOs by Year of Establishment

Table-4.1.5: Distribution of NGOs by Number of Employees

S. No.	*Number of Employees*	*Frequency*	*Percentage (%)*
1.	<15	52	53
2.	16 – 30	29	29
3.	>30	18	18
	Total	**99**	**100**

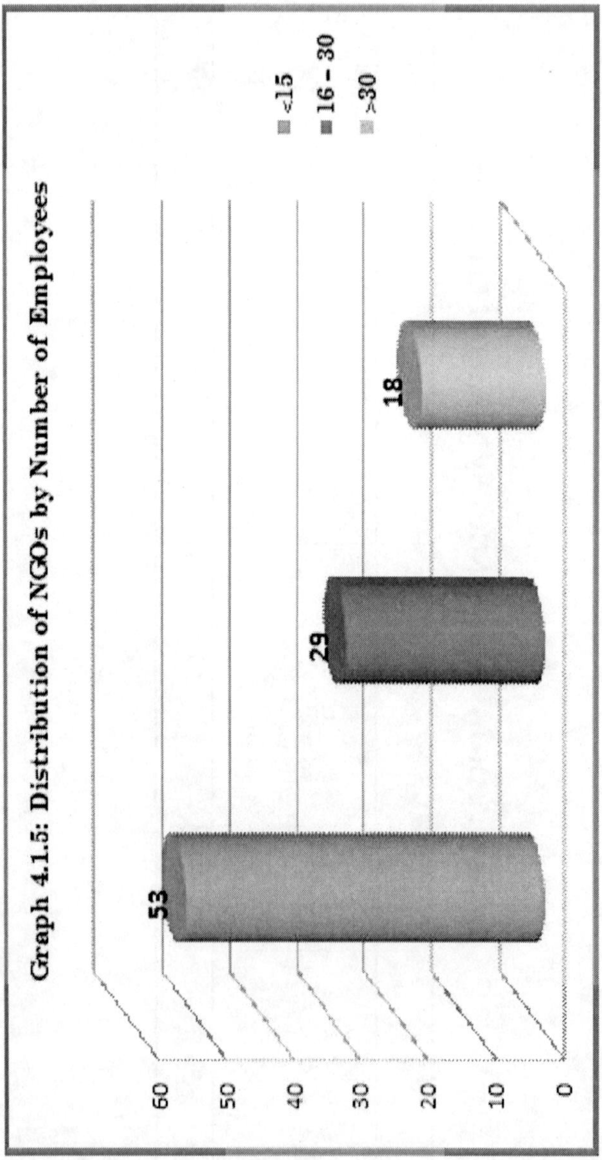

Graph 4.1.5: Distribution of NGOs by Number of Employees

less than 15 employees whereas 18 per cent of NGOs are having more than 30 employees the remaining 29 per cent of NGOs have the employees, between 16-30.

The following Table 4.1.6 and graphical presentation shows that majority (48 per cent) of NGOs are working in the mandals between 5-10 whereas 20 per cent of NGOs are working in more than 10 mandals, the remaining 32 per cent of NGOs are working in less than 5 mandals.

The following Table 4.1.7 and graphical presentation shows that the majority (31 per cent) of NGOs are focused at the area of Economy whereas 8 per cent of NGOs focused at Human Rights, the remaining 30 per cent are at Education, 17 per cent are at Health, 10 per cent are at Environment and 3 per cent are at other focused areas.

The following Table 4.1.8 and graphical presentation shows that the majority (45 per cent) of NGOs are receiving funds from State Government whereas 6 per cent of NGOs are receiving from multi- national companies, the remaining 20 per cent are from Central Government and 19 per cent are from both state and central governments and 10 per cent are from International Organizations.

The following Table 4.1.9 and graphical presentation shows that the majority (53 per cent) of NGOs are having their annual budget between 5-10 lakhs whereas 7 per cent of NGOs are having between 16-20 and above 20 another 7 per cent lakhs. The remaining 33 per cent of NGOs are receiving funds between 11-15 lakhs.

The following Table 4.1.10 and graphical presentation shows that the majority social workers (70 per cent) are Un-trained whereas 30 per cent of Social workers are trained. It is noted that many NGOs has the requirement of professionally trained and skilled staff members.

The following Table 4.1.11 and graphical presentation shows that the majority (94 per cent) of NGOs do not have their website whereas 6 per cent of NGOs have their website.

Table-4.1.6: Distribution of NGOs by Coverage of Revenue Mandals in Vizianagaram District

S. No.	*No. of Mandals Covered*	*Frequency*	*Percentage (%)*
1.	< 5	32	32
2.	5-10	48	48
3.	>10	19	20
	Total	**99**	**100**

Graph 4.1.6: Distribution of NGOs by Coverage of Revenue Mandals in Vizianagaram District

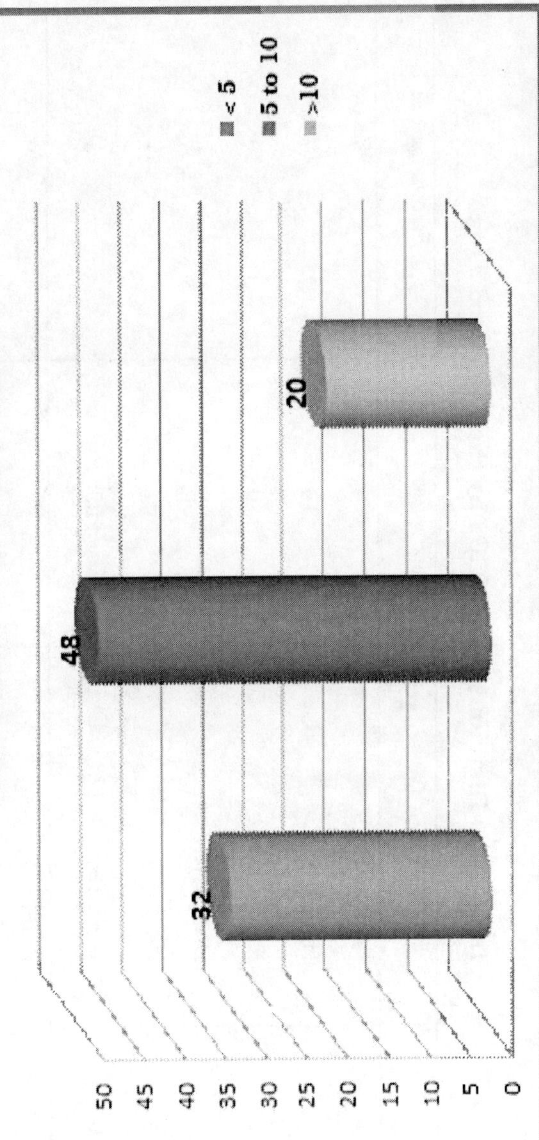

Table-4.1.7: Distribution of NGOs by their Focused Area

S. No.	*Focused Area*	*Frequency*	*Percentage (%)*
1.	Education	30	30
2.	Health	16	17
3.	Environment	10	10
4.	Human Rights	08	8
5.	Economy	31	31
6.	Any Other	03	3
	Total	**99**	**100**

Graph 4.1.7: Distribution of NGOs by their Focused Area

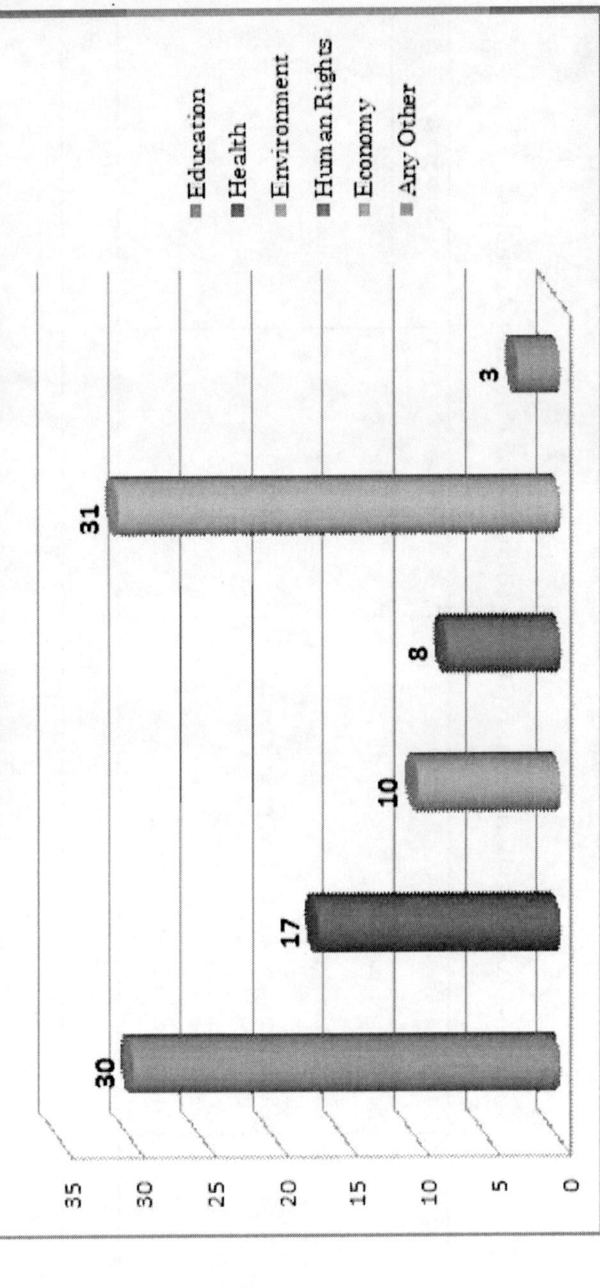

Table-4.1.8: Distribution of NGOs by their Major Funding Agencies

S. No.	*Major funding Agencies*	*Frequency*	*Percentage*
1.	State Government	45	45
2.	Central Government	20	20
3.	Both State and the Central governments	19	19
3.	International Organisations	10	10
4.	Multinational Companies	05	6
	Total	99	100

Graph 4.1.8: Distribution of NGOs by their Major Funding Agencies

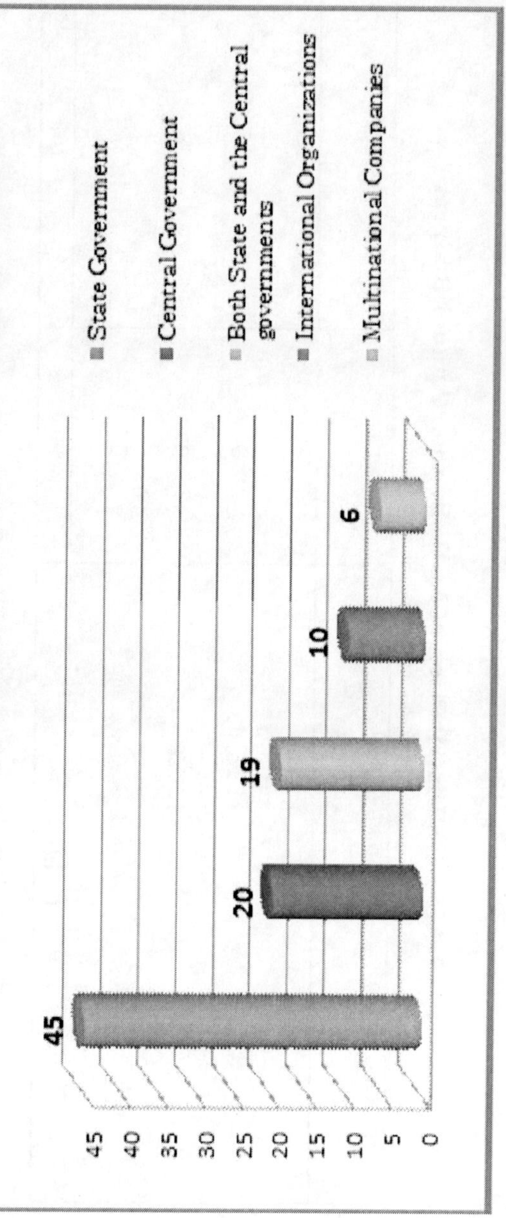

Table-4.1.9: Distribution of NGOs by their Annual Budgets

S. No.	*Annual Budget (Rs. In Lakhs)*	*Frequency*	*Percentage (%)*
1.	5 – 10	53	53
2.	11-15	32	33
3.	16-20	07	7
4.	20 and above	07	7
	Total	**99**	**100**

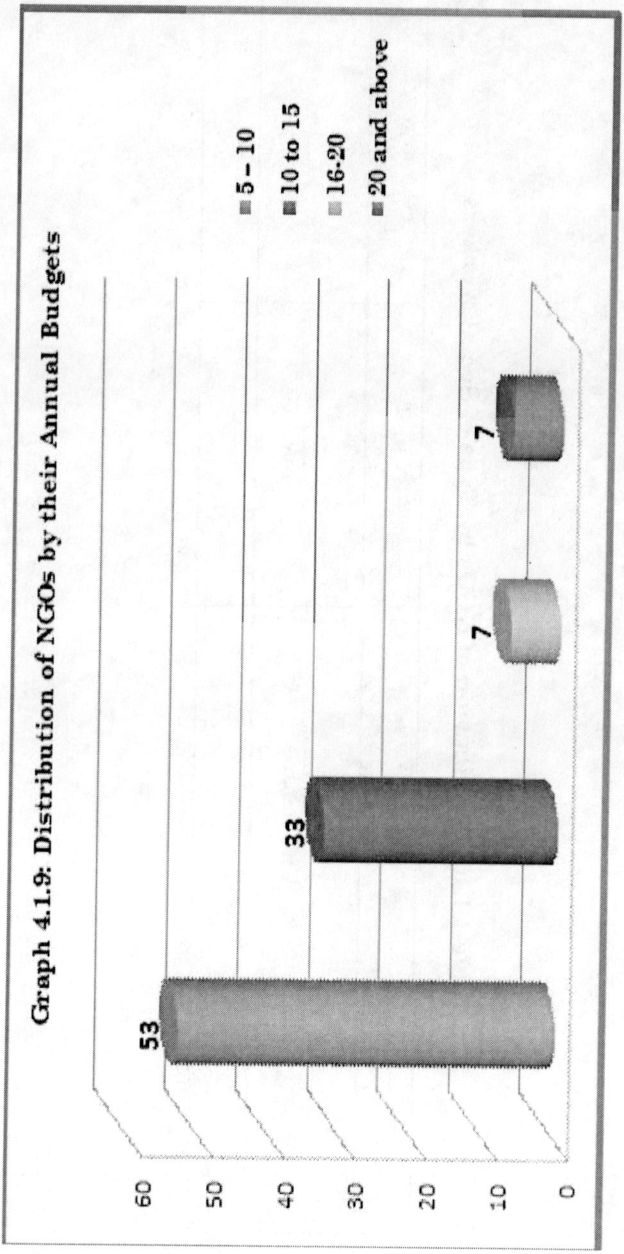

Graph 4.1.9: Distribution of NGOs by their Annual Budgets

Table-4.1.10: Distribution of NGOs by Type of Social Workers

S. No.	*Type of Social Worker*	*Frequency*	*Percentage (%)*
1.	Trained	29	30
2.	Un-Trained	70	70
	Total	**99**	**100**

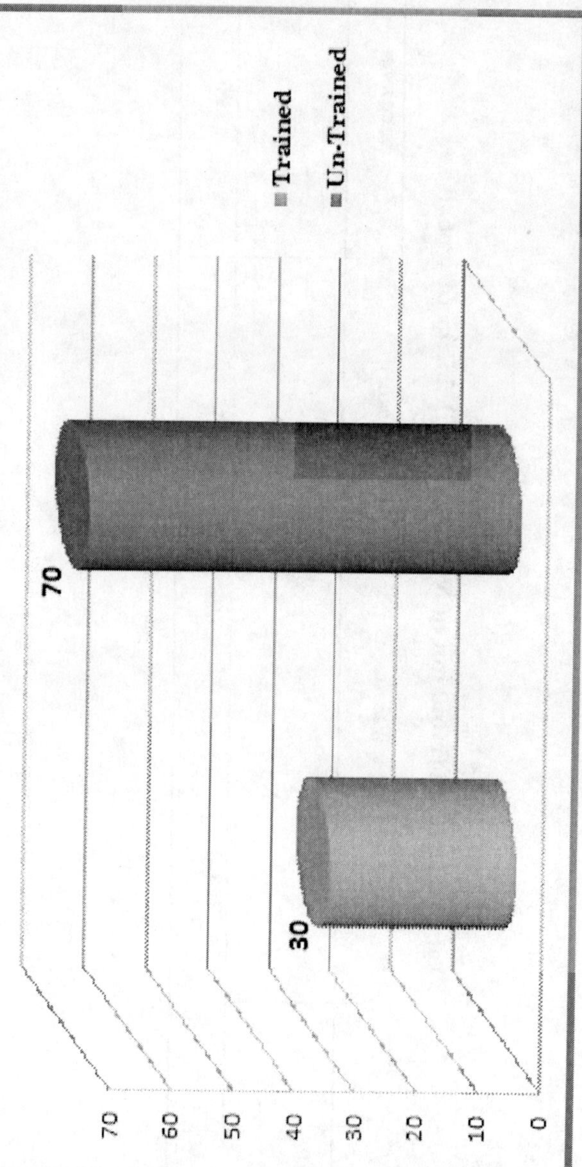

Graph 4.1.10: Distribution of NGOs by Type of Social Workers

Table-4.1.11: Distribution of NGOs by Availability of website

S. No.	*Availability of Website*	*Frequency*	*Percentage*
1.	Yes	5	6
2.	No	94	94
	Total	**99**	**100**

Graph 4.1.11: Distribution of NGOs by Availability of website

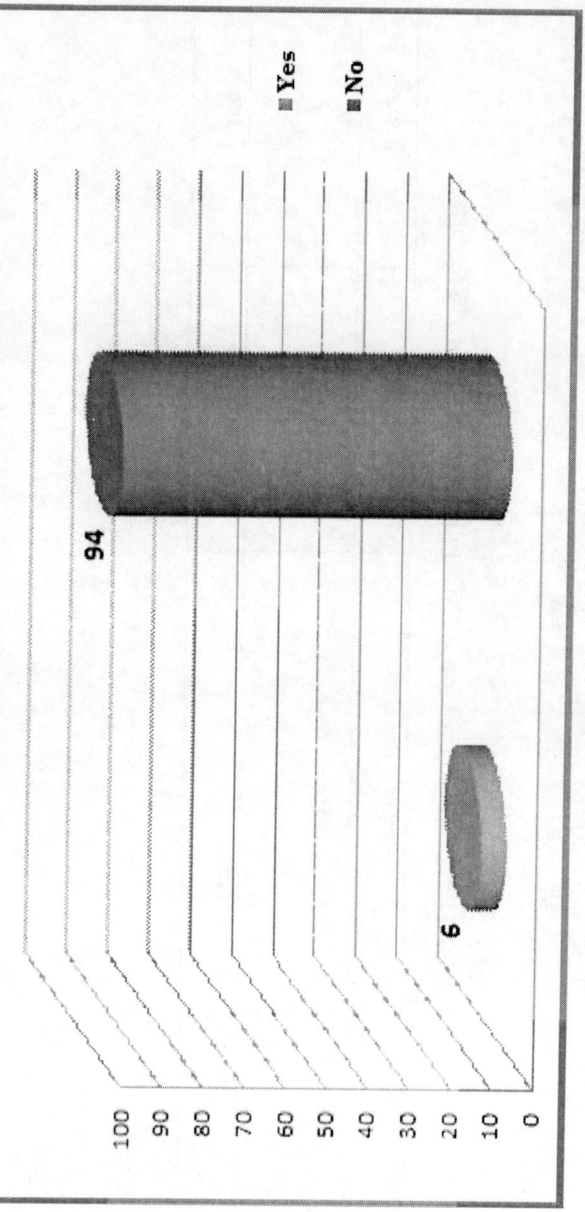

Table-4.1.12: Distribution of NGOs by Location of Head Office

S. No.	*Location of Head Office*	*Frequency*	*Percentage (%)*
1.	District Head Quarters	31	32
2.	Operational Area	68	68
	Total	**99**	**100**

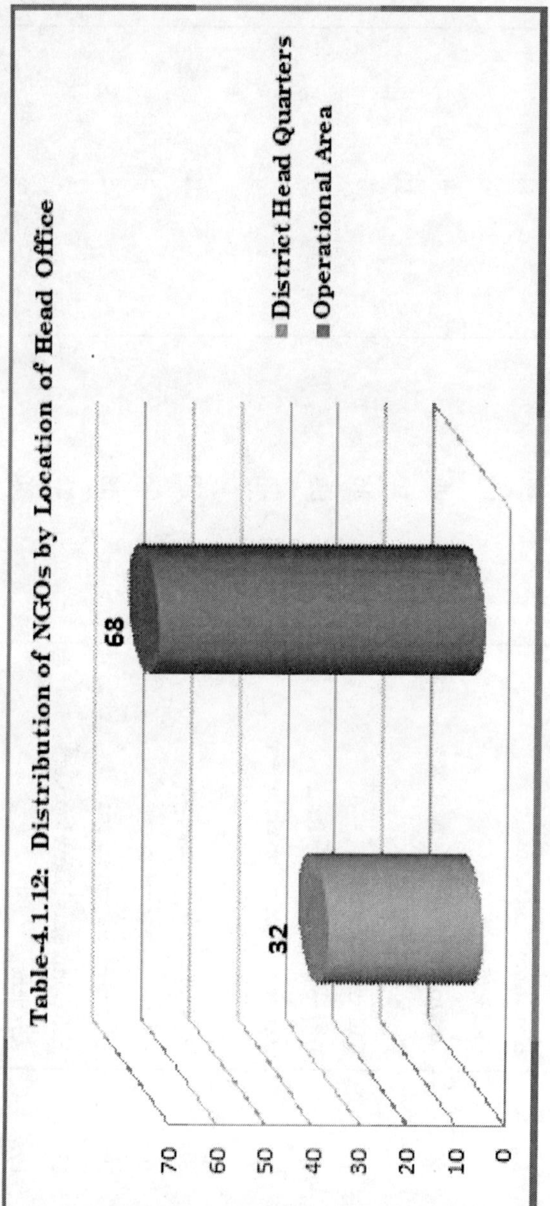

Table-4.1.12: Distribution of NGOs by Location of Head Office

Table-4.1.13: Distribution of NGOs by their Opinions towards Key Achievements

S. No.	*Key Achievement*	*Frequency*	*Percentage (%)*
1.	Economic Sustainability	12	13
2.	Self Efficacy	06	6
3.	Improved Health Conditions	08	8
4.	Capacity Building	10	10
5.	Cultural Change	06	6
6.	Improve in Literacy Rate	09	9
7.	Participationin Development Activities	09	9
8.	Awareness in all aspects	10	10
9.	Women Empowerment	08	8
10.	Livestock improvement	08	8
11.	Environmental Development	05	5
12.	Advocacy	08	8
Total		**99**	**100**

Table-4.1.13: Distribution of NGOs by their Opinions towards Key Achievements

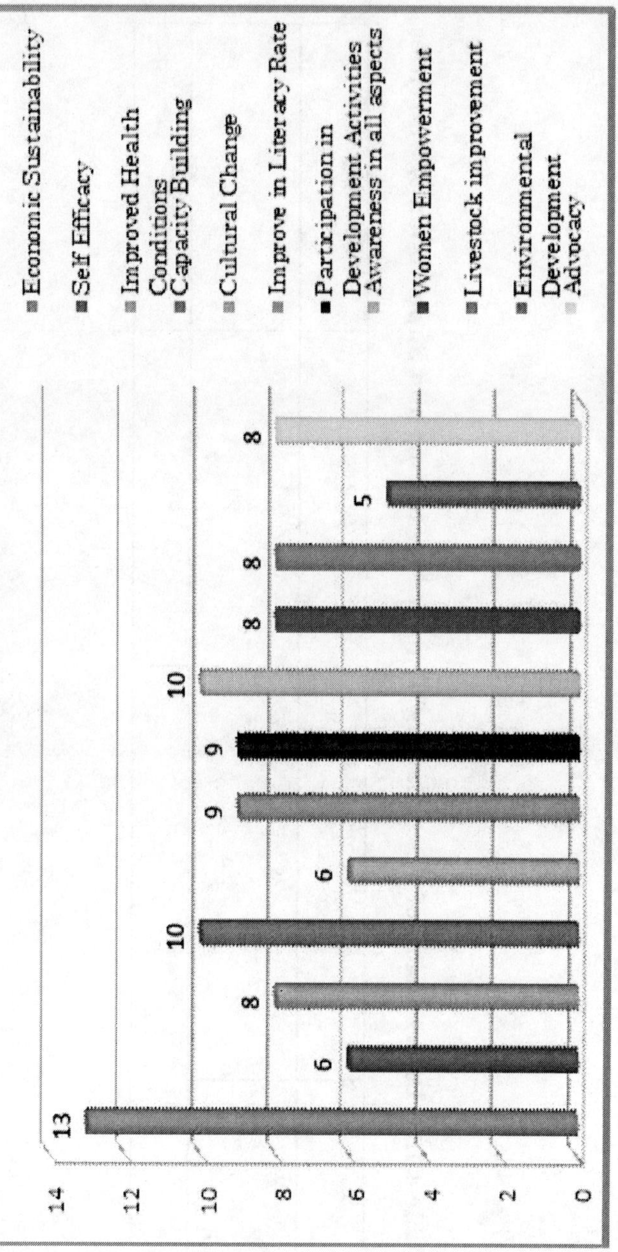

Table-4.1.14: Distribution of NGOs having Regular Monitoring and Supervision of Activities

S. No.	*Regular Monitoring and Supervision*	*Frequency*	*Percentage (%)*
1.	Yes	75	75
2.	No	24	25
	Total	**99**	**100**

Graph 4.1.14: Distribution of NGOs having Regular Monitoring and Supervision Activities

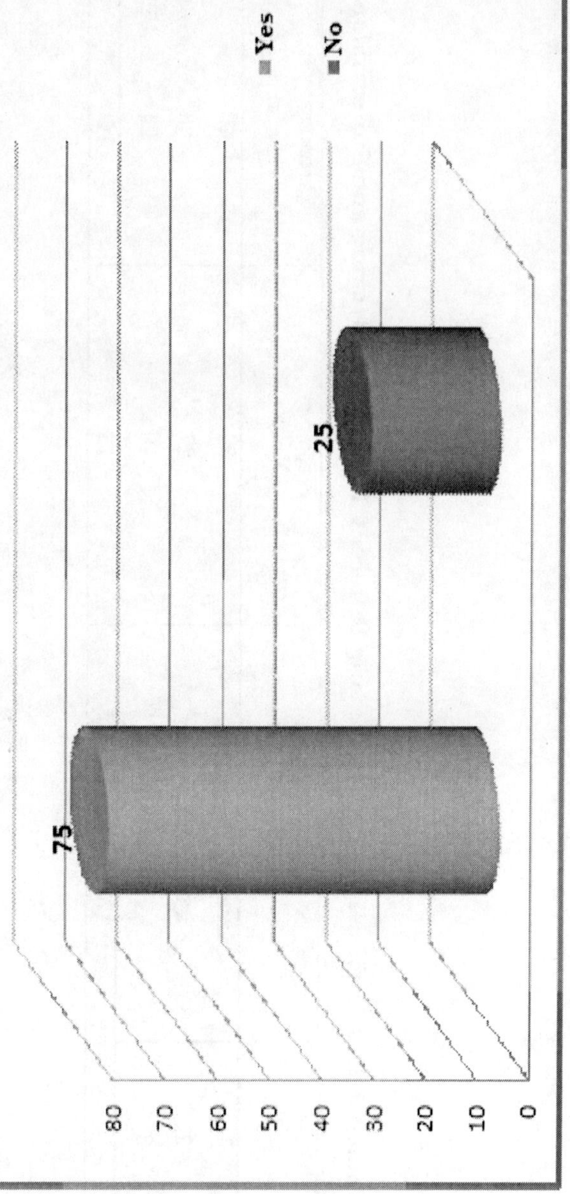

Table-4.1.15: Distribution of NGOs having Different Types of Monitoring and Supervision

S. No.	*Type of Monitoring and Supervision*	*Frequency N=75*	*Percentage (%)*
1.	Internal Monitoring	30	40
2.	External Monitoring	27	36
3.	Both	18	24
	Total	**75**	**100**

Graph 4.1.15: Distribution of NGOs having Different Types of Monitoring and Supervision

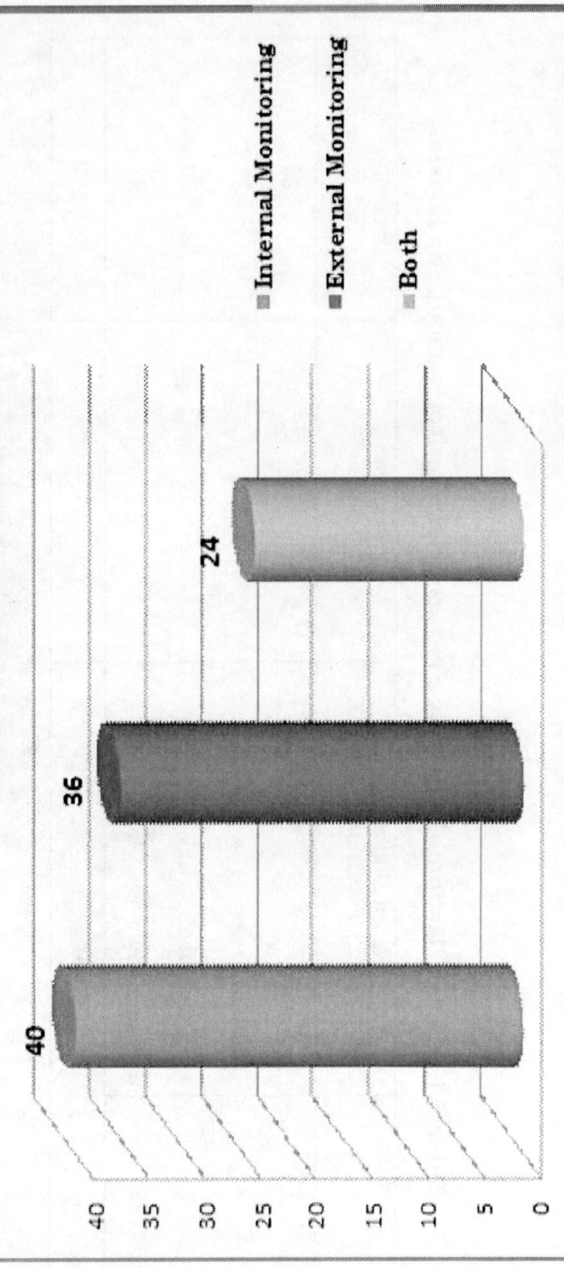

Table-4.1.16: Distribution of NGOs by Frequency of Monitoring and Supervision

S. No.	*Frequency of Monitoring and supervision*	*Frequency N=75*	*Percentage (%)*
1.	Monthly	15	20
2.	Bi-monthly	25	33
3.	Quarterly	12	16
4.	Annually	23	31
	Total	**75**	**100**

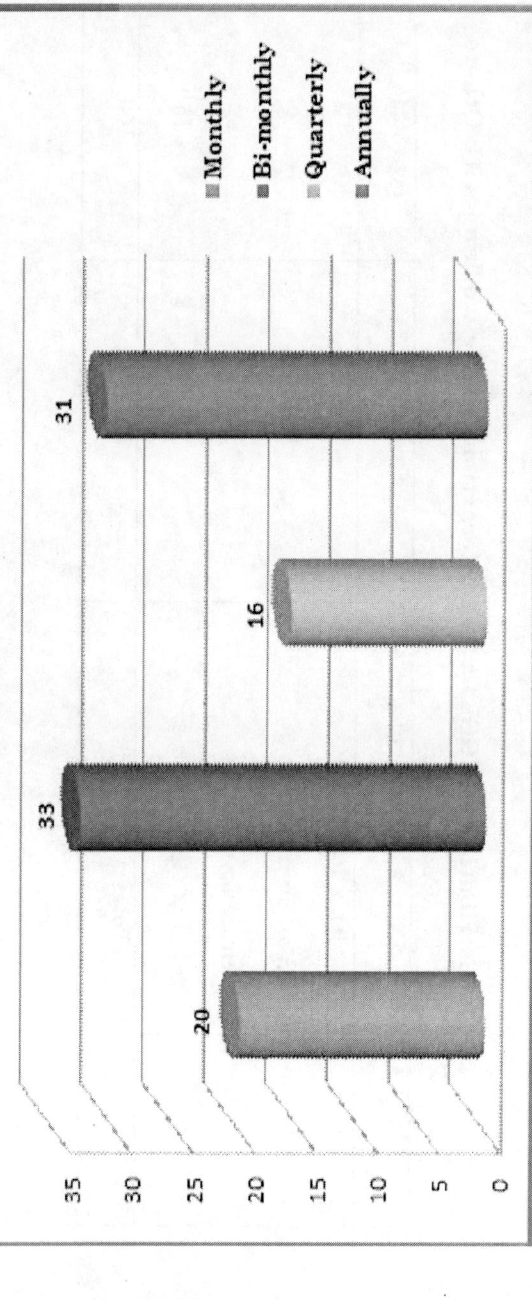

Graph 4.1.16: Distribution of NGOs by Frequency of Monitoring and Supervision

Table-4.1.17: Distribution of NGOs having Interaction and Networking with Others

S. No.	*Networking Institution*	*Frequency*	*Percentage (%)*
1.	Academic Institutions	15	15
2.	State Government	59	60
3.	Central Government	10	10
4.	Other NGOs	15	15
	Total	**99**	**100**

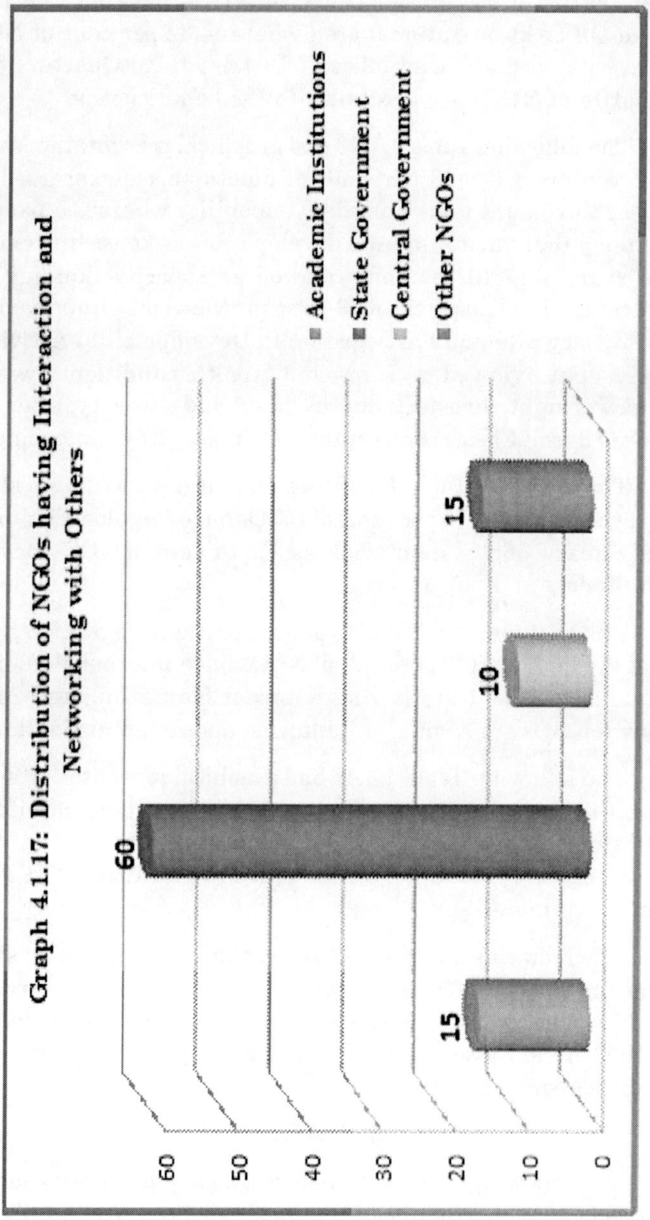

Graph 4.1.17: Distribution of NGOs having Interaction and Networking with Others

The following Table 4.1.12 and graphical presentation shows that the majority (68 per cent) of NGOs have located their Head Office at operational area whereas 32 per cent of NGOs have located their head office at District Head Quarters .The majority of NGOs are accessible to the beneficiaries.

The following Table 4.1.13 and graphical presentation shows that the majority (13 per cent) of functionaries expressed the key achievement is economic sustainability whereas 5 per cent opinined that environmental development as key achievement, the remaining 10 per cent viewed as capacity Building and awareness in all aspects and 9 per cent viewed as Improvement in Literacy rate and Participation in Developmental Activities, 8 per cent viewed as improved Health conditions, women empowerment, livestock improvement and advocacy, 6 per cent viewed as self Efficacy and Cultural change as Key Achievements.

The following Table 4.1.14 and graphical presentation shows that the majority (75 per cent) of NGOs have Regular Monitoring and Supervision System whereas 25 per cent of NGOs have no monitoring and Supervision.

The following Table 4.1.15 and graphical presentation shows that the majority (40 per cent) of NGOs have Internal Monitoring while 36 per cent are having External Monitoring and 24 per cent of NGOs are having both Internal and External Monitoring.

The following Table 4.1.16 and graphical presentation shows that the majority (33 per cent) of NGOs has their monitoring and supervision once in two months whereas 16 per cent have quarterly and remaining 31 per cent have annually and 20 per cent have monthly.

The following Table 4.1.17 and graphical presentation shows that the majority (60 per cent) of NGOs have their Interaction and Network with State Government whereas 10 per cent have with Central Government and the remaining 15 per cent have with Academic institutions and with other NGOs.

SECTION-II

The following Table 4.2.1 and graphical presentation focuses on socio-economic profile of beneficiaries. So, variables like Age

Table 4.2.1: Socio-economic Profile of Beneficiaries

Particulars	*Frequency*	*% Values*
Age Group		
18-28	464	46.87
29-38	276	27.88
39-48	196	19.80
49 and above	54	5.4
Total	**990**	**100**
Type of Family		
Joint	464	46.87
Nuclear	526	53.13
Total	**990**	**100**
Caste		
OC	63	6.37
SC	529	53.43
ST	136	13.74
BC	262	26.46
Total	**990**	**100**

Particulars	*Frequency*	*% Values*
Religion		
Hindu	629	63.54
Muslim	132	13.33
Christian	229	23.13
Total	**990**	**100**
Education		
Illiterate	462	46.67
Primary	349	35.25
High School	120	12.12
Intermediate	44	4.44
Graduate and Above	15	1.52
Total	**990**	**100**
Income (Rs.) per month		
Below 1000	205	20.71
1001-2000	414	41.82
2001-3000	279	28.18
3000 and above	92	9.29
Total	**990**	**100**

Graph : 4.2.1

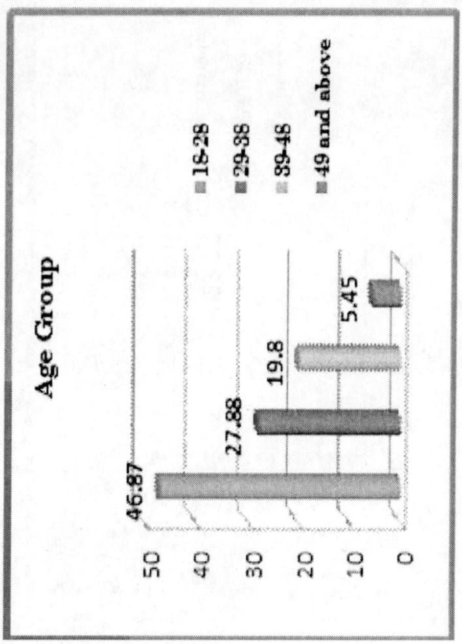

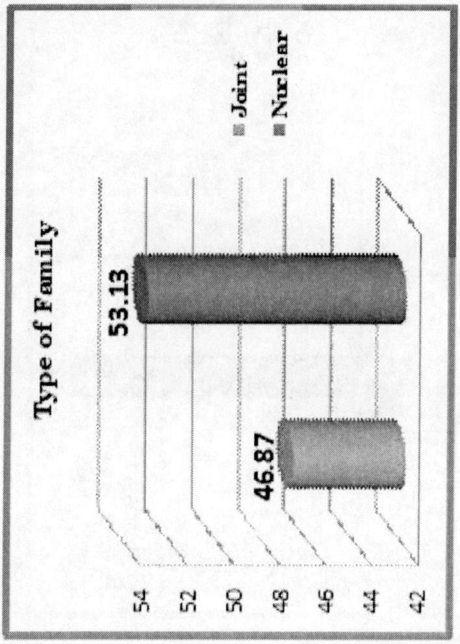

(Contd.)

(Contd. Graph 4.2.1)

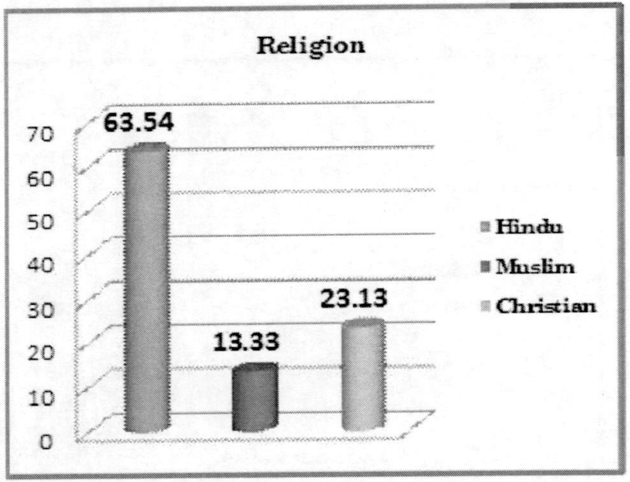

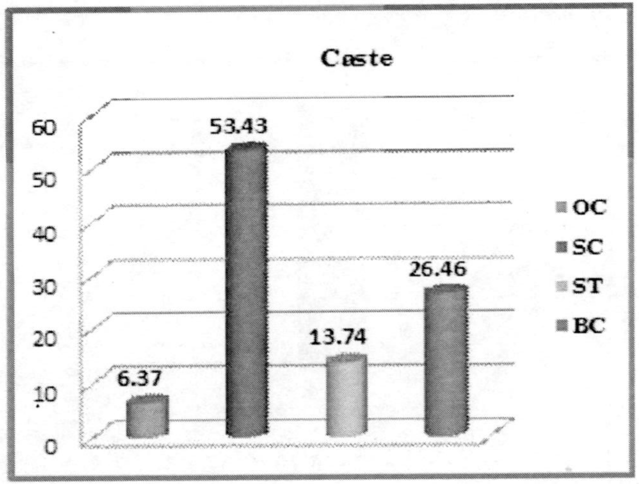

(Contd.)

(Contd. Graph 4.2.1)

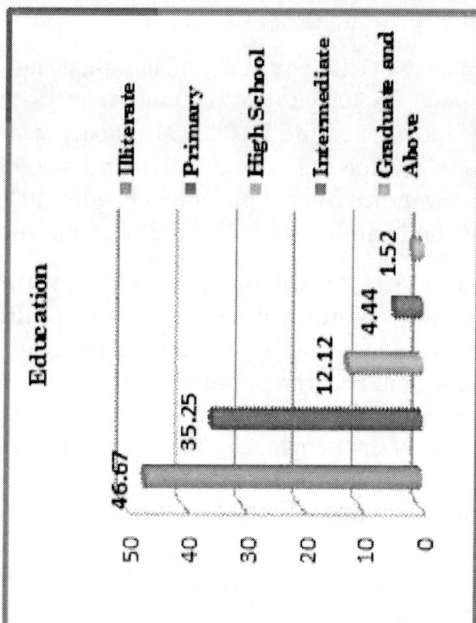

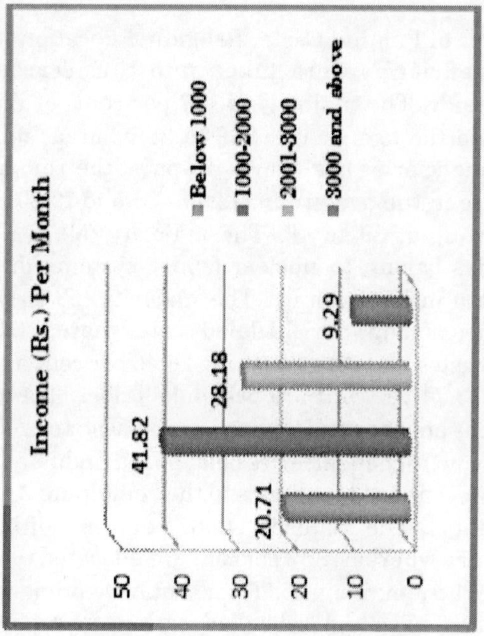

Group, Type of Family, Caste, Religion, Education and Income of the beneficiaries were taken into consideration for the research study. The majority (46.87 per cent) of Beneficiaries are between the age group of 18 to 28 whereas only 5.45 per cent of Beneficiaries are above 49 years, the remaining 27.88 per cent are in the age group of 29 to 38 and 19.80 per cent in the age group of 39 to 48. The majority (53.13 per cent) of beneficiaries belong to nuclear family system whereas 46.87 per cent are in joint family. The majority (53.43 per cent) of beneficiaries belongs to Scheduled caste whereas 6.37 per cent are other castes and the remaining 26.46 per cent are backward caste and 13.74 per cent are Schedule Tribes. The most of the beneficiaries are poor and having low social status. The majority (63.54 per cent) of beneficiaries belongs to Hindu Religion where as 13.33 per cent are Muslims and the remaining 23.13 per cent are Christians. The majority (46.67 per cent) of beneficiaries are illiterates whereas 1.52 per cent are educated till graduation and above, the remaining 35.25 per cent have primary education, 12.12 per cent have high school education and 4.44 per cent are educated till intermediate.

The majority (41.82 per cent) of beneficiaries are having Income between Rs.1001 to Rs.2000 per month whereas 9.29 per cent are having income Rs.3000 and above, the remaining 28.18 per cent are having income between Rs.2001 to Rs.3000 and 20.71 per cent are having income below Rs. 1000. It is clear that most of the beneficiaries are from below poverty line.

Concept and Understanding of the Development:

Development is multi dimensional and multi faced. All human beings have to satisfy material, cultural, social and spiritual needs, and it is the purpose of development strategies and policies to contribute to their fulfillment. Development must serve the needs of the people, especially the poor, which means the needs must be factored into development strategies. These must be designed to address the issue squarely: not as a hoped-for secondary fall-out or an afterthought, but as the centerpiece of development thinking. Development does not always take into account human values and social goals; rather, development is often confused with economic growth.

Table 4.2.2 : Distribution of Beneficiaries by their opinion on their Development of Life

S. No	Opinion on Development of Life	Frequency	Percentage
1.	Developed	259	26.17
2.	Partially developed	636	64.24
3.	Low Developed	95	9.59
	Total	**990**	**100**

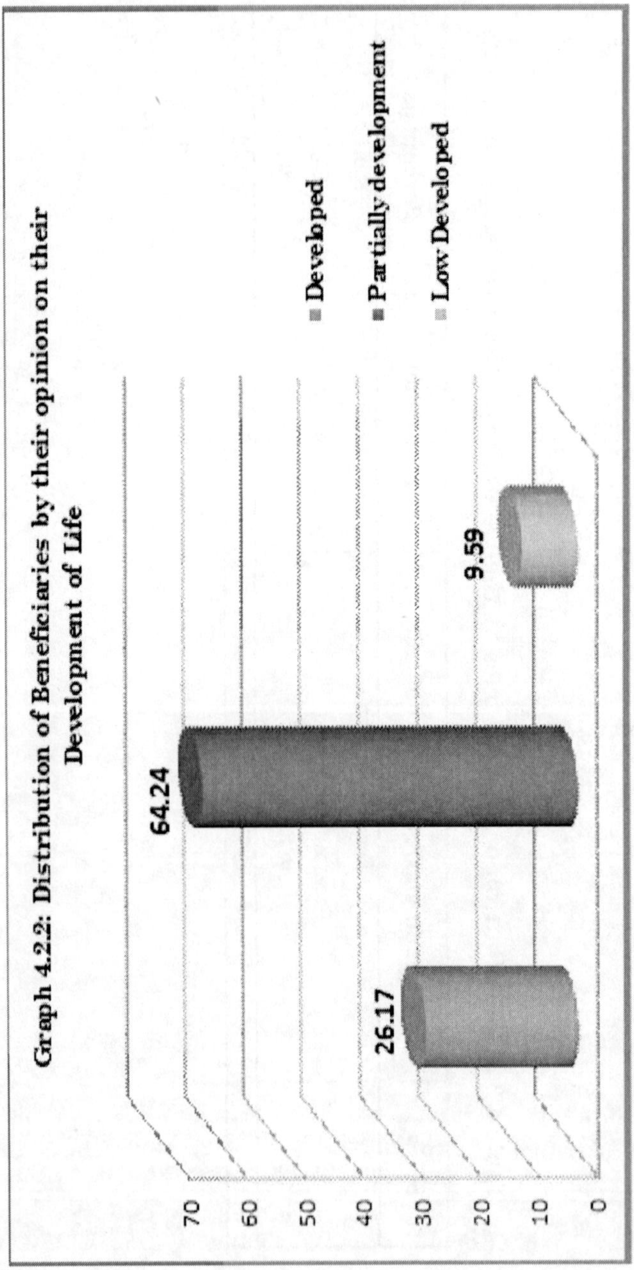

Graph 4.2.2: Distribution of Beneficiaries by their opinion on their Development of Life

Table 4.2.3: Distribution of Beneficiaries by their opinion in Development in various Aspects.

S.No	*Development in various aspects*	*Frequency N=990*	*Percentage*
1.	Social Development	827	83.54
2.	Economic development	919	92.83
3.	Political development	649	65.56
4.	Cultural & Religious development	497	50.20

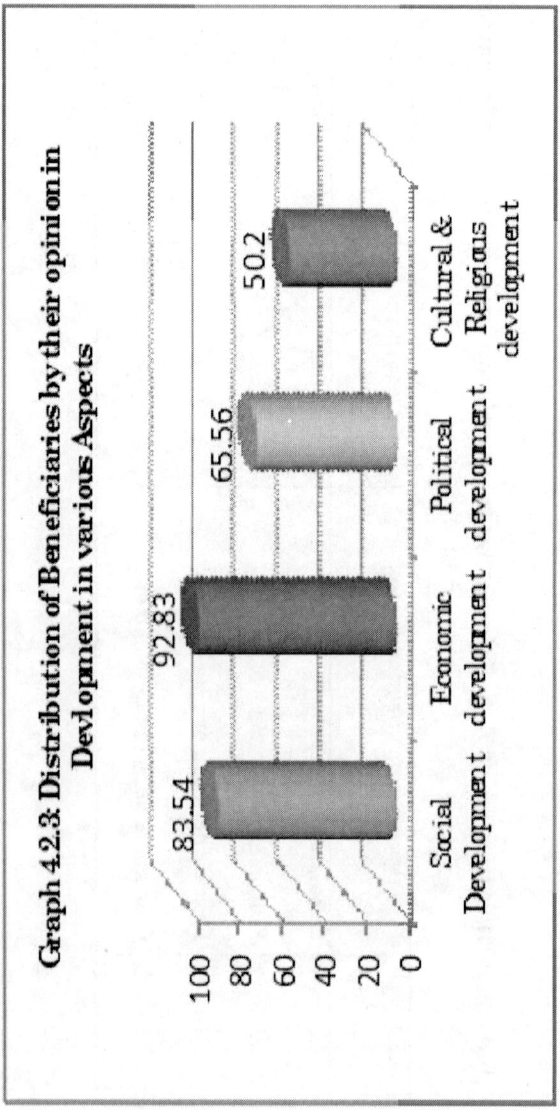

Graph 4.2.3: Distribution of Beneficiaries by their opinion in Devlopment in various Aspects

Stavenhagen also say that development however defined, must be considered not only as a process of accumulation or change, but rather as a collective good, to the extent that it addresses the common needs of specific social and cultural groups. Sometimes the development, itself is the problem, when it is imposed without taking into account the particularities of specific contexts. Stavenhagen maintains that development policies designed to alleviate poverty, overcome social exclusion and reduce persistent categorical inequalities so it must focus on the needs and rights of specific categories or groups in the society. But they must do so in areas that make a deference; that is , productive activities, and the ownership and control of the means of production and the fruits oflabour, the organization of the workface, decision-making processes, legal framework enabling autonomous participation, respect for cultural differences and social identities and, of course democratic governance. The development concept is interrelated and interlinked with social, economic, political, cultural and religious aspects of life.

The following Table 4.2.2 andgraphical presentation explains on the opinion of the beneficiaries on their development of life. The majority (64.24 per cent) of beneficiaries expressed that they have developed partially in all aspects of their life. Whereas 9.59 per cent expressed that they have low development. The remaining 26.17 per cent have expressed that they developed in all aspects of life.

The following Table 4.2.3 and graphical presentation indicates that the majority (92.83 per cent) have expressed their opinion that economic development is the major change in their life. Whereas 50.20 per cent have expressed regarding cultural and religious development, the remaining 83.54 per cent on social development and 65.56 per cent on political development. It is noted that most of the beneficiaries expressed that they developed in social and economic aspects when compared with other developments.

Social Development:

"Social Development is the promotion of a sustainable society that is worthy of human dignity by empowering marginalized groups, women and men, to undertake their own development, to improve their social and economic position and to acquire their rightful in society" (Bilance). "Social development is equally of social opportunities" (Amartya Sen). "Human development is a process of enlarging peoples" choices. The most critical choice that people should have, include a long and healthy life, access to knowledge and income, assets and employment for a decent standard of living. But human development concerns more than the formation of human capabilities such as improved health or knowledge. It also concerns the use of these capabilities" (India Human Development Report, 1999)

Education plays an important role in the process of social development. Education that liberates and promotes better option of life, then everyone lives with dignity and confidence.

In this, it deals with various elements of social development as viewed by the beneficiaries. Such as infrastructural development, practice of social evils, improvement of education, status of women, level of self image , awareness on various laws related to better life and their knowledge on health facilities.

The following Table 4.2.4 and graphical presentation reveals that the majority (89.49 per cent) of beneficiaries viewed that infrastructural development has taken place. Whereas 10.51 per cent have expressed that there is no infrastructural development.

The following Table 4.2.5 and graphical presentation shows that the majority (87.27 per cent) have expressed that they are not practising any type of social evils. Whereas 12.73 per cent of beneficiaries expressed that they are practising some social evils.

The following Table 4.2.6 and graphical presentation shows that the majority (56.26 per cent) of respondents expressed that they are improved in their education. Whereas 11.82 per cent have expressed that there is no improvement in their education. The remaining 32.42 per cent have expressed that they have partial improvement in their education.

Table 4.2.4: Distribution of Beneficiaries by their opinion on infrastructural development

S. No	*Opinion on Infrastructural development*	*Frequency*	*Percentage*
1.	Yes	886	89.49
2.	No	104	10.51
	Total	990	100

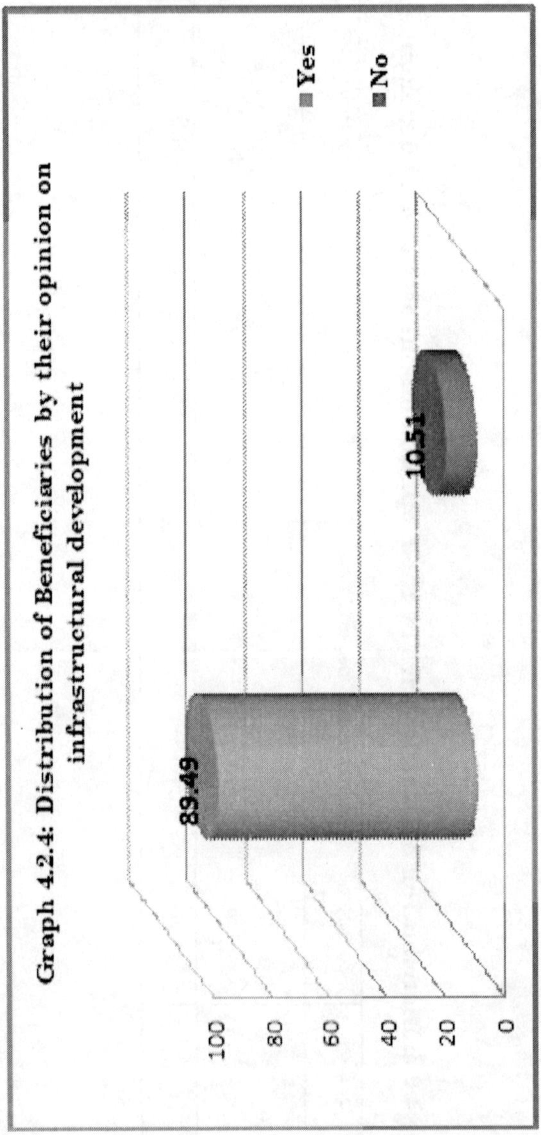

Graph 4.2.4: Distribution of Beneficiaries by their opinion on infrastructural development

Table 4.2.5: Distribution of Beneficiaries by their practice of Social evils

S.No	*Practice of Social evils*	*Frequency*	*Percentage*
1.	Yes	126	12.73
2.	No	864	87.27
	Total	**990**	**100%**

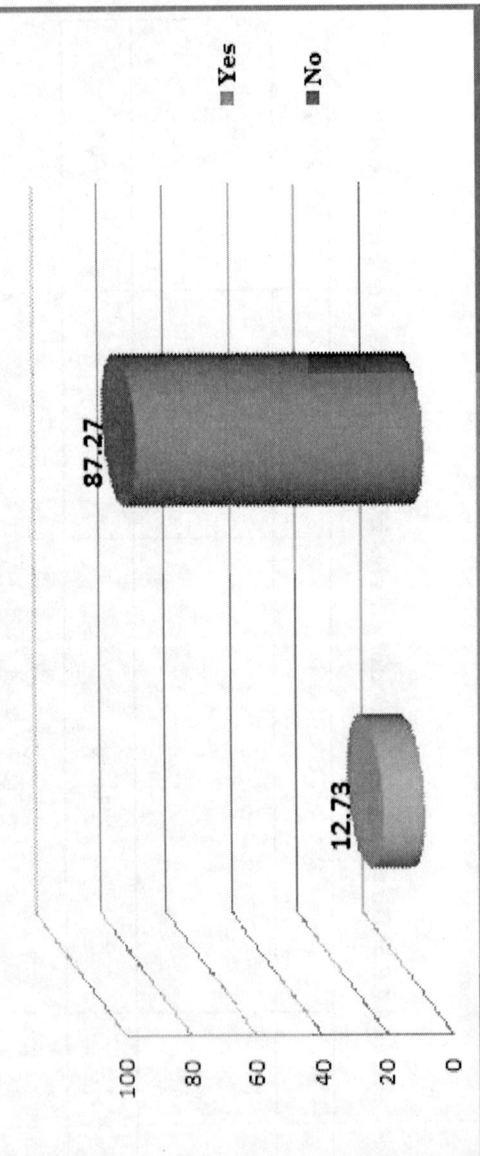

Graph 4.2.5: Distribution of Beneficiaries by their practice of Social evils

Table 4.2.6: Distribution of Beneficiaries by their opinion on improvement of Education

S.No	*Opinion on Improvement Education*	*Frequency*	*Percentage*
1.	Improved	557	56.26
2.	Partiallyimproved	321	32.42
3.	Not Improved	112	11.32
	Total	**990**	**100**

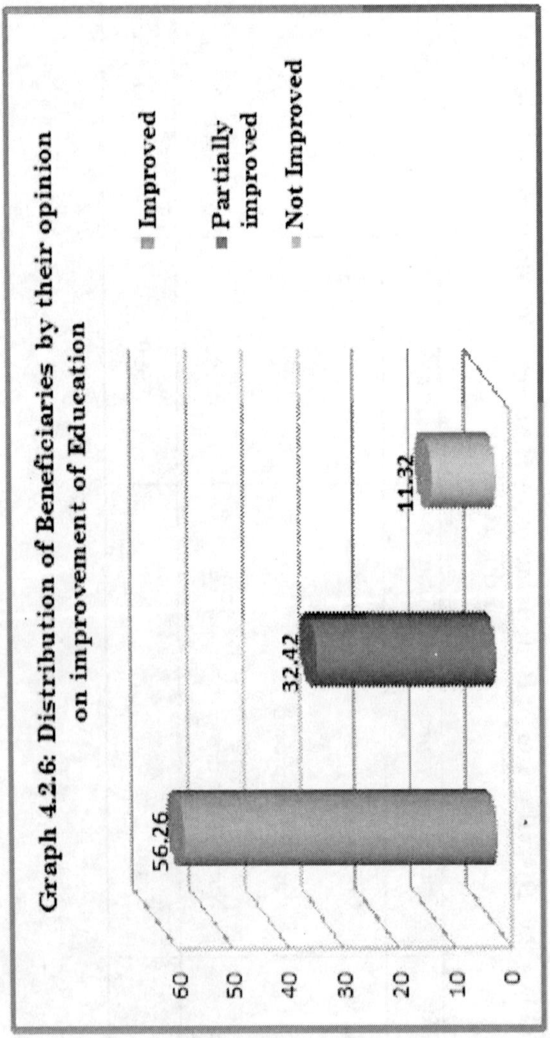

Graph 4.2.6: Distribution of Beneficiaries by their opinion on improvement of Education

Table 4.2.7: Distribution of Beneficiaries by their opinion on the status of women

S.No	*Opinion on Status of Women*	*Frequency*	*Percentage*
1.	Improved	537	54.24
2.	Partially improved	342	34.55
3.	Not Improved	111	11.21
	Total	**990**	**100**

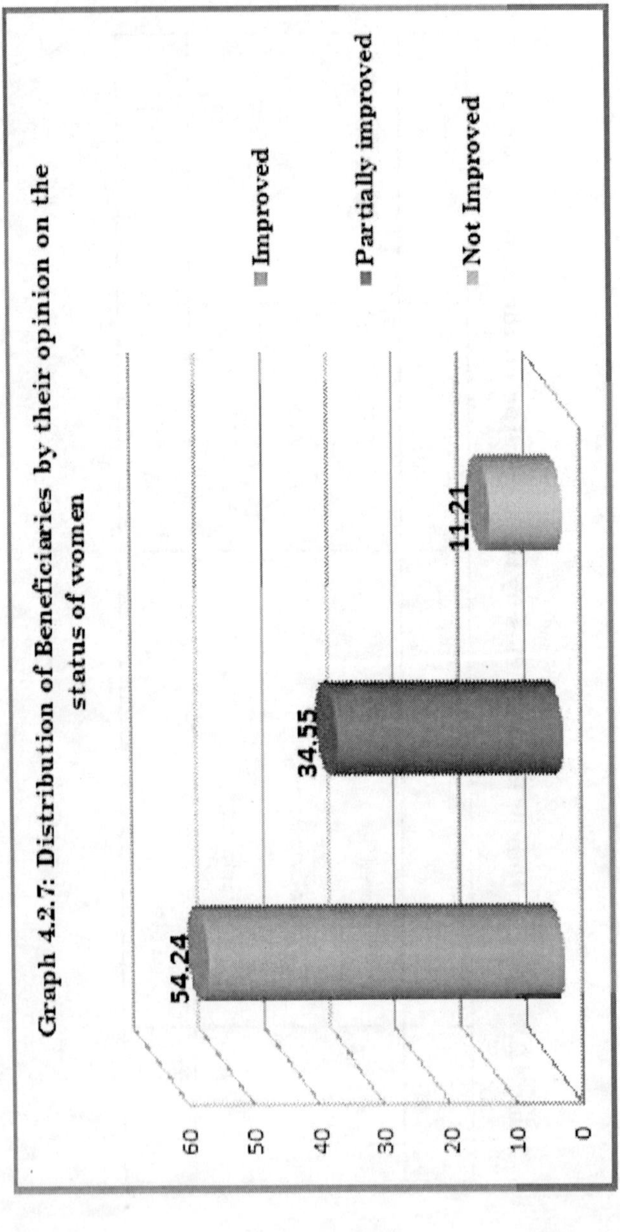

Graph 4.2.7: Distribution of Beneficiaries by their opinion on the status of women

Table 4.2.8: Distribution of Beneficiaries by their opinion on the level of self image

S.No	*Opinion on the level of Self image*	*Frequency*	*Percentage*
1.	Improved	645	65.15
2.	Partially improved	243	24.55
3.	Not Improved	102	10.30
	Total	**990**	**100**

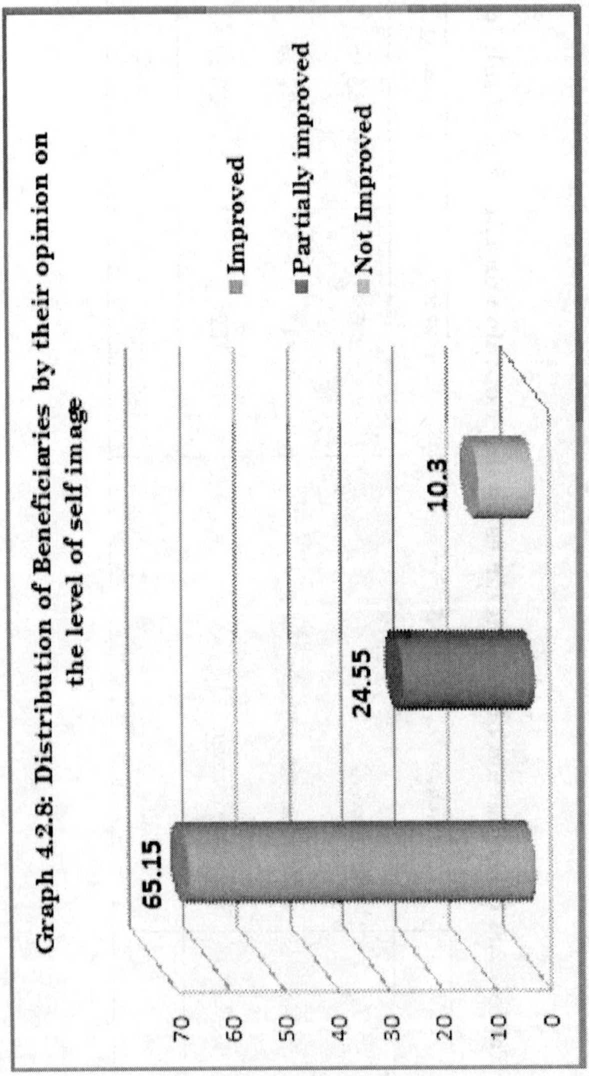

Graph 4.2.8: Distribution of Beneficiaries by their opinion on the level of self image

Table 4.2.9: Distribution of Beneficiaries by their level of awareness on various laws related to life

S.No	*Level of awareness on laws*	*Frequency*	*Percentage*
1.	High	634	64.04
2.	Middle	233	23.54
3.	Low	123	12.42
	Total	**990**	**100**

Graph 4.2.9: Distribution of Beneficiaries by their level of awareness on various laws related to life

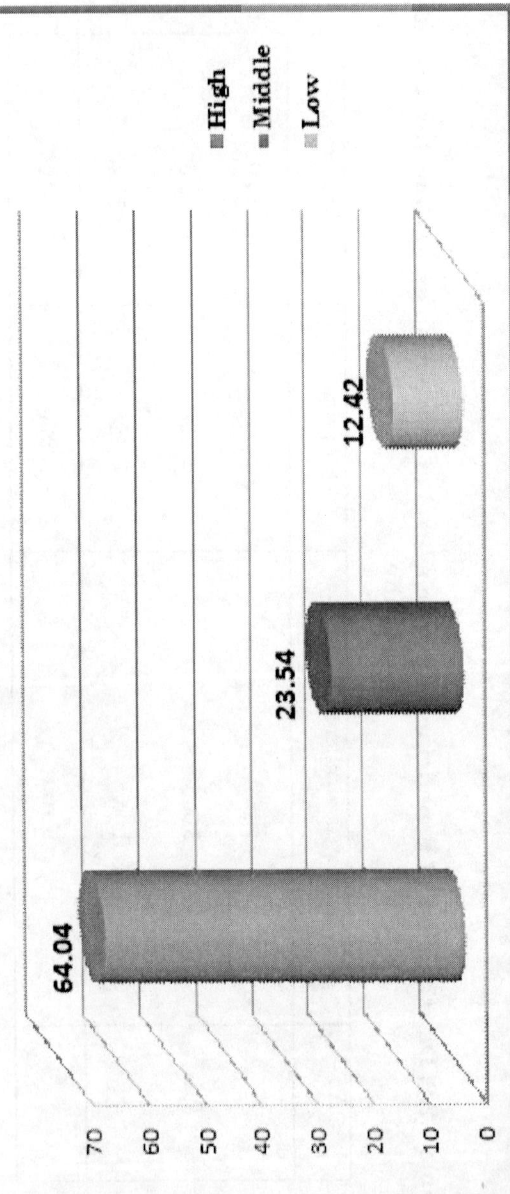

Table 4.2.10: Distribution of Beneficiaries by their knowledge on Health facilities

S. No	*Knowledge on Health facilities*	*Frequency*	*Percentage*
1.	Yes	886	89.49
2.	No	104	10.51
	Total	**990**	**100**

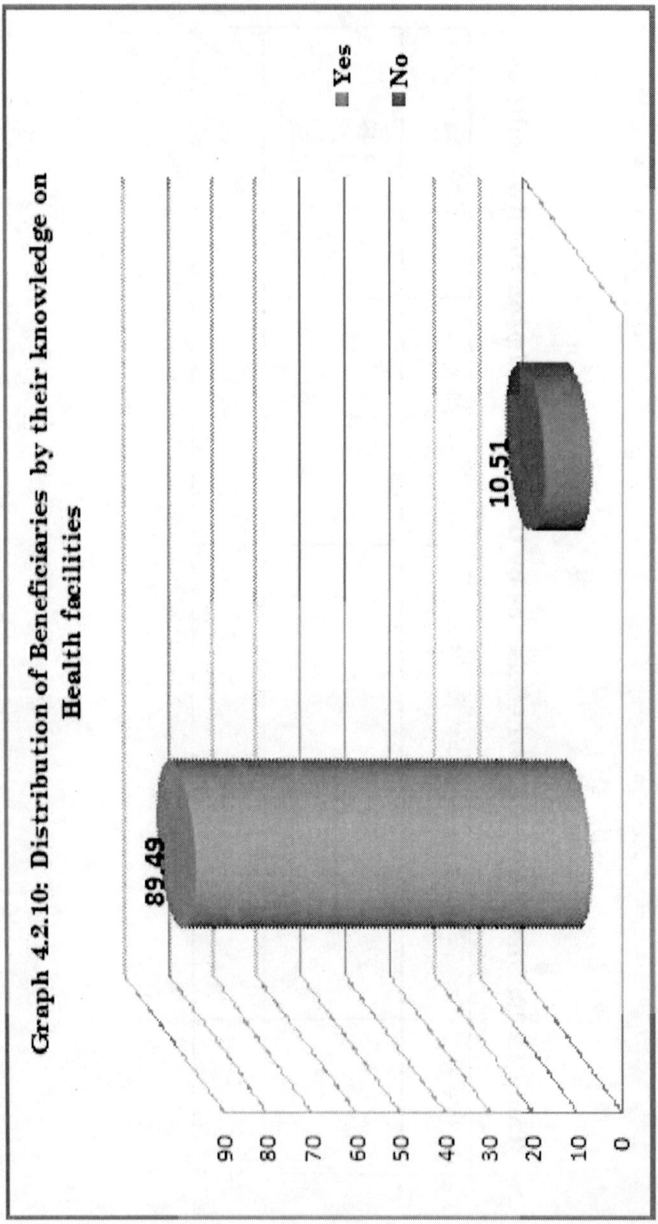

Graph 4.2.10: Distribution of Beneficiaries by their knowledge on Health facilities

The following Table 4.2.7 and graphical presentation shows that the majority (54.24 per cent) of beneficiaries viewed that status of women is improved. Whereas 11.21 per cent have expressed that there is no improvement in the status of women. The remaining 34.55 per cent have expressed that there is a partial improvement in the status of women.

The following Table 4.2.8 and graphical presentation indicates that the majority (65.15 per cent) have expressed that their self image is very much gained and improved. Whereas 10.30 per cent have expressed that they have no self image. The remaining 24.55 per cent expressed that their self image is partially improved.

The following Table 4.2.9 and graphical presentation indicates that the majority (64.04 per cent) have expressed that they are aware of the laws related to life for better standards of living. Whereas 10.42 per cent have expressed that they have low level of awareness on laws. The remaining 23.54 per cent have expressed that they have average knowledge on laws.

The following Table 4.2.10 and graphical presentation reveals that the majority (89.49 per cent) of beneficiaries are aware of all the health facilities. Whereas 10.59 per cent have expressed that they do not have any kind of awareness or knowledge on health facilities.

Economic Development

Economic development can be seen as a complex multi-dimensional concept involving improvements in human well-being. The importance of non economic aspects like more leisure time, access to health education, environment, freedom or justice. Economic growth is a necessary but insufficient condition for economic development. Economic development is about outcomes of development occurs with the deduction and elimination of poverty, inequality and unemployment with in a growing economy (Dudley seers). The main objectives of economic development are producing more life sustaining necessities such as food, shelter & health care and broadening their distribution raising standards of living and individual self esteem. Expanding economic and social choice and reducing fear (Michael Todaro). Economic development as it can lead to improve standard of living through job creation, higher income, better education and additional social services. According to A.K.Sen's 'Capabilities Approach' to development, typically, income transfers through the government sector are insignificant in developing countries. Therefore, the only way that poverty can be reduced and basic needs met is by increasing the availability or reduction in the under-utilization of labour and reducing poverty, improving the provision of basic needs, goods and services and, at least to some extent, reducing inequalities in income distribution should be incorporated. Mostly NGOs deals with the people who are below poverty line. They are economically very low and exploited at all levels.

In this, it deals with economic development of beneficiaries by knowing various elements of economic matters such as savings in the Bank, knowledge in availing bank loan, increasing of assets and livestock, position of self reliance, and experience in financial exploitation. And improvement on their level of income.

The following Table 4.2.11 and graphical presentation indicates that the majority (90.81 per cent) of beneficiaries have their savings in the bank. Whereas 9.19 per cent have no savings in the bank. The significant number of respondents are aware of savings in the bank for their economical development.

The following Table 4.2.12 and graphical presentation indicates that the majority (90.61 per cent) of respondents have expressed that they have knowledge of availing bank loans and also bank transactions. Whereas 9.39 per cent do not have any knowledge on bank transactions.

The following Table 4.2.13 and graphical presentation reveals that the majority (69.6 per cent) have expressed that they have partially increased their assets and livestock. Whereas 6.56 per cent have expressed that they do not have any assets. The remaining 23.84 per cent of respondents have increased their assets and live stock for better standard of life.

Table 4.2.11: Distribution of Beneficiaries by their savings in the Bank

S.No.	*Savings in the Bank*	*Frequency*	*Percentage*
1.	Yes	899	90.81
2.	No	91	9.19
	Total	**990**	**100**

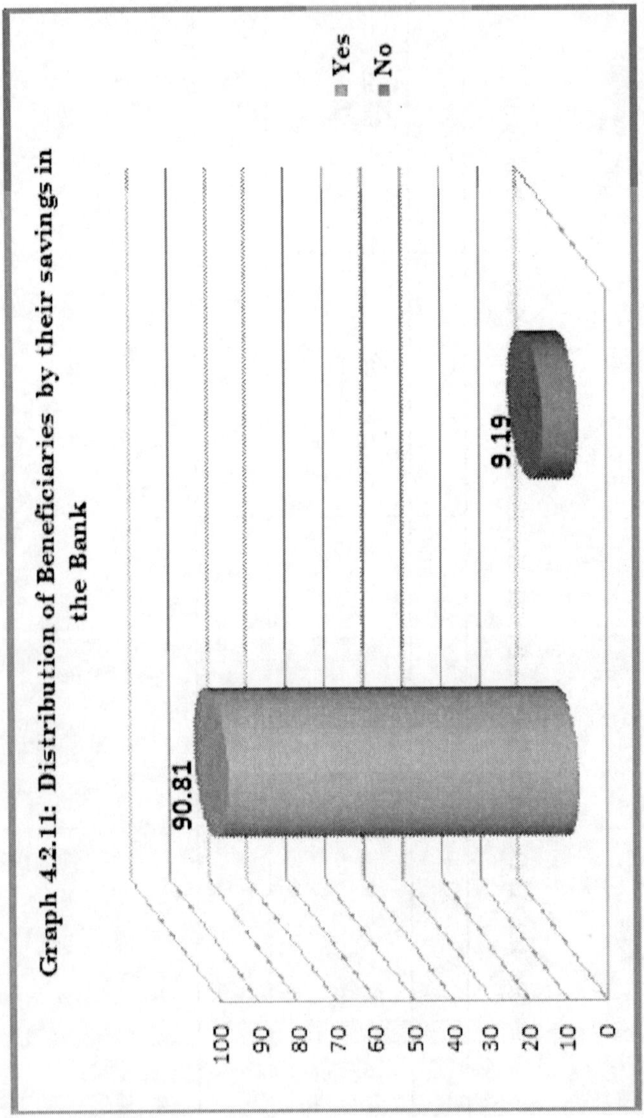

Graph 4.2.11: Distribution of Beneficiaries by their savings in the Bank

Table 4.2.12: Distribution of Beneficiaries by their knowledge in availing bank loans

S.No.	*Knowledge in availing bank loan*	*Frequency*	*Percentage*
1.	Yes	897	90.61
2.	No	93	9.39
	Total	**990**	100

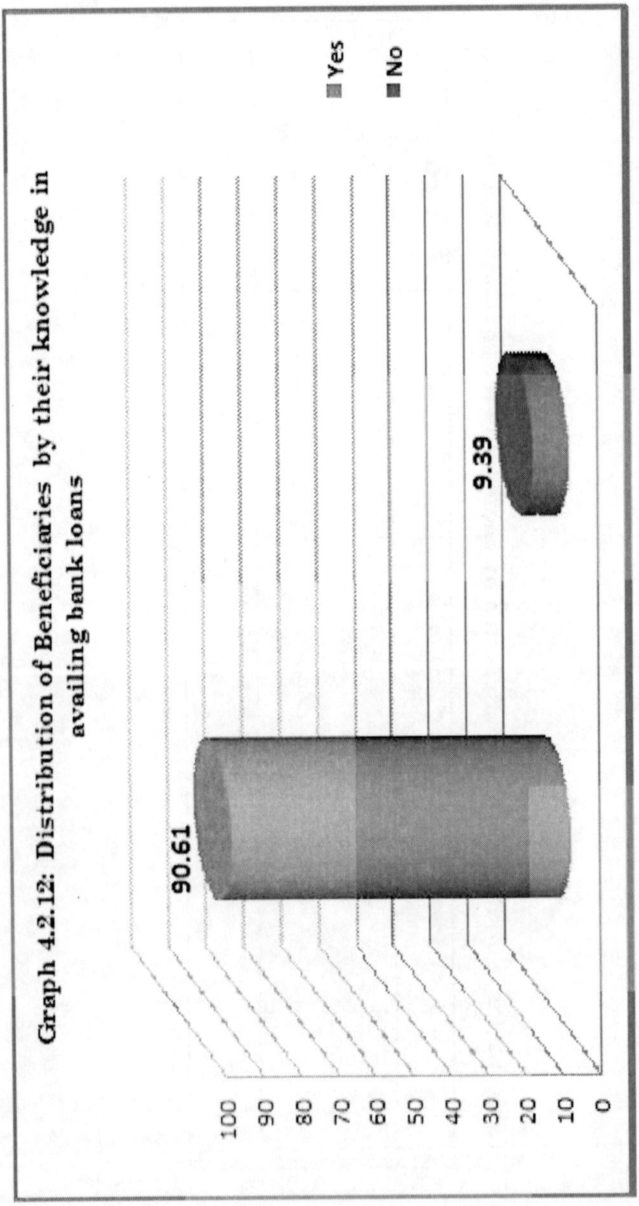

Graph 4.2.12: Distribution of Beneficiaries by their knowledge in availing bank loans

Table 4.2.13: Distribution of Beneficiaries by their increase of assets and livestock

S. No.	*Opinion on increase of assets and livestock*	*Frequency N=990*	*Percentage*
1.	Increased	236	23.84
2.	Partially increased	689	69.60
3.	Not increased	65	6.56
	Total	**990**	**100**

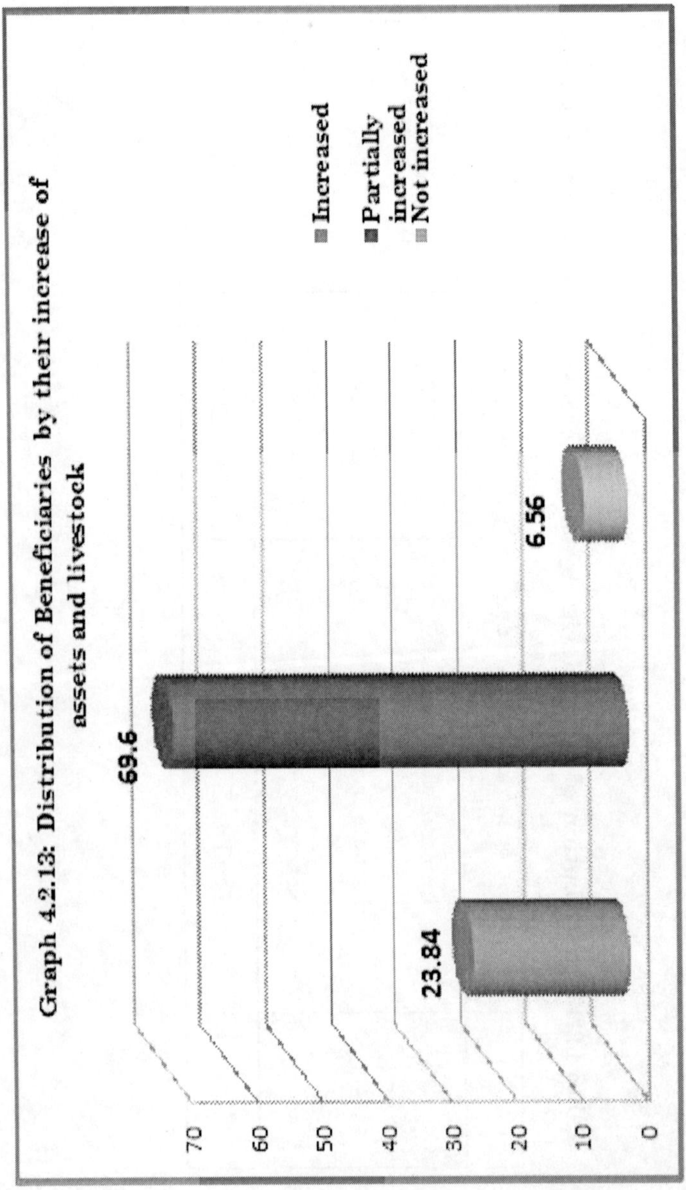

Graph 4.2.13: Distribution of Beneficiaries by their increase of assets and livestock

Table 4.2.14: Distribution of Beneficiaries by their position of self reliance

S. No.	*Position of self reliance*	*Frequency*	*Percentage*
1.	Yes	875	88.38
2.	No	115	11.62
	Total	**990**	**100**

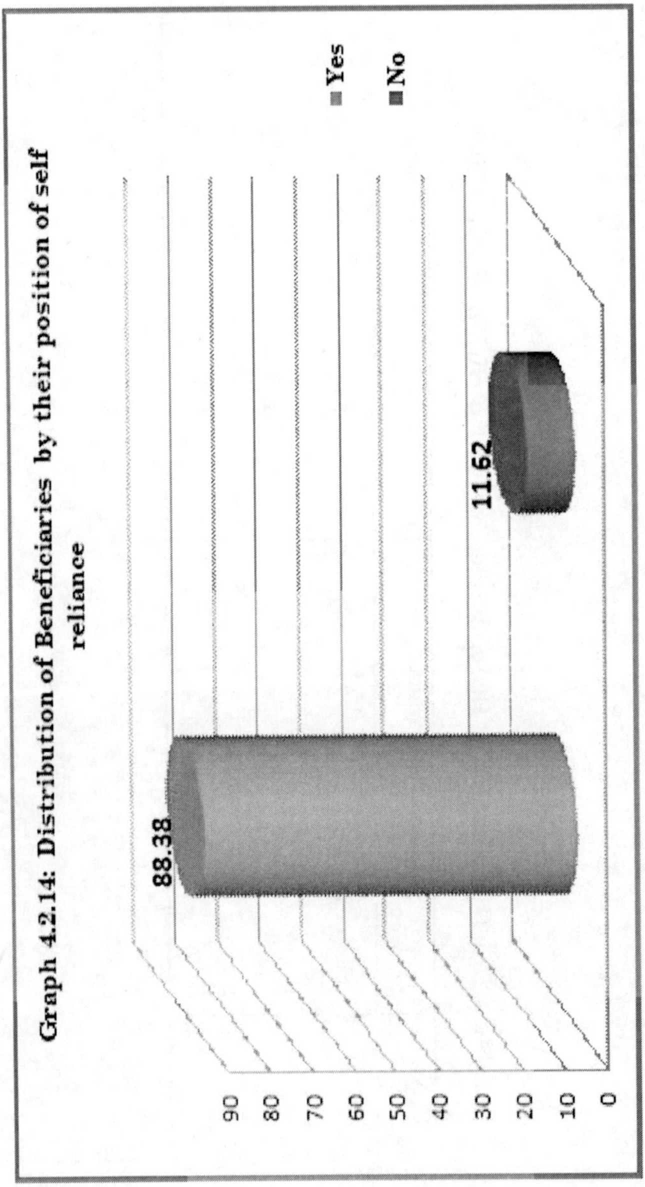

Graph 4.2.14: Distribution of Beneficiaries by their position of self reliance

Table 4.2.15: Distribution of Beneficiaries by their opinion on experience in financial exploitation

S. No.	*Opinion on experience in financial exploitation*	*Frequency*	*Percentage*
1.	High	42	4.24
2.	Average	302	30.51
3.	Not at all	646	65.25
	Total	**990**	**100**

Graph 4.1.15: Distribution of NGOs having Different Types of Monitoring and Supervision

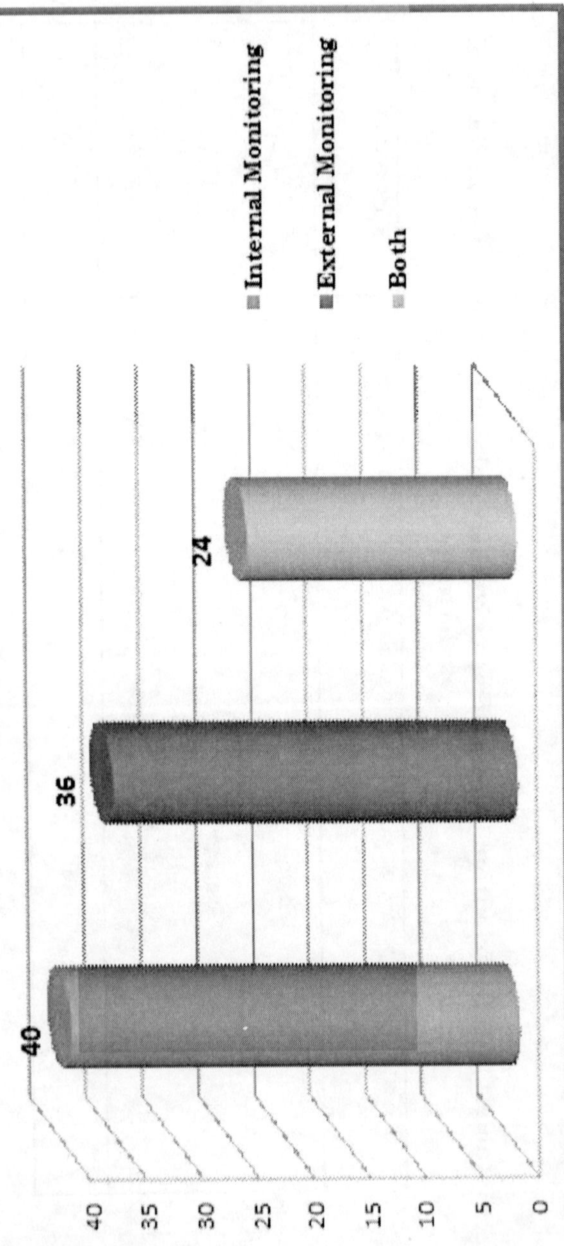

Table 4.2.16: Distribution of Beneficiaries by their improvement on level of income

S. No.	*Improvement on level of income*	*Frequency*	*Percentage*
1.	Improved	744	75.15
2.	Partially Improved	202	20.41
3.	Not Improved	44	4.44
	Total	**990**	**100**

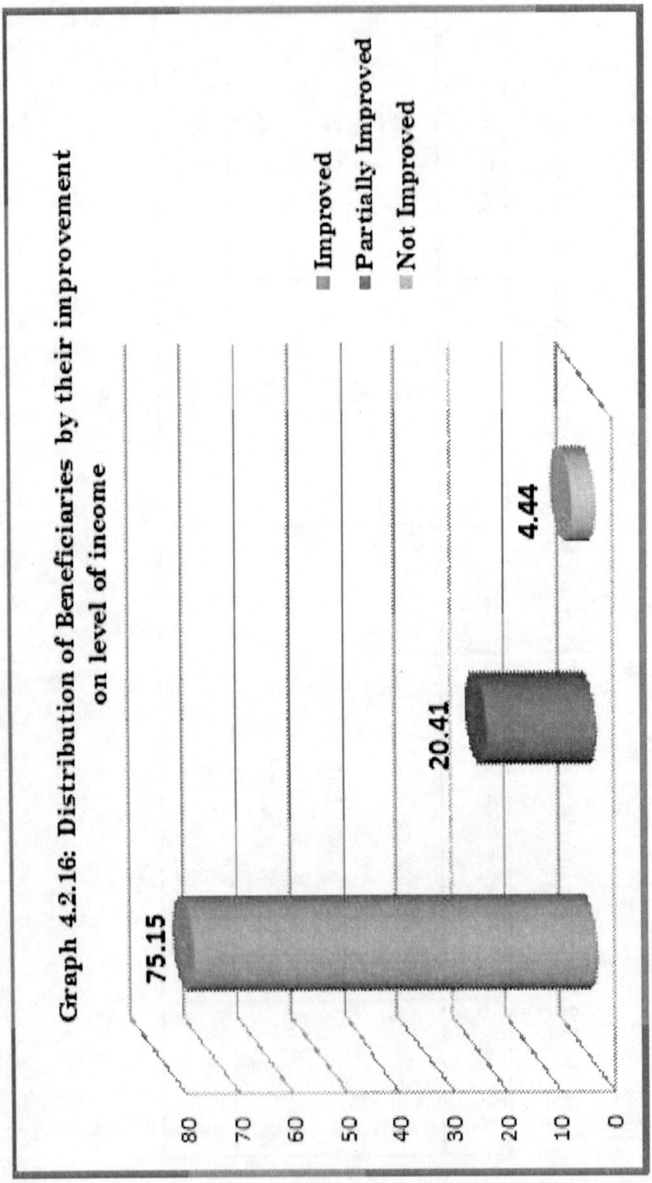

Graph 4.2.16: Distribution of Beneficiaries by their improvement on level of income

The following Table 4.2.14 and graphical presentation shows that the majority (88.38 per cent) of respondents are selfreliant. Whereas 11.62 per cent are not self reliant. The significant number of respondents are independent in their financial position.

The following Table 4.2.15 and graphical presentation shows that the majority (65.25 per cent) of respondents have expressed that they have not experienced any financial exploitation. Whereas 14.24 per cent of respondents have experienced financial exploitation. The remaining 30.51 per cent are expressed that they experienced financial exploitation sometimes.

The following Table 4.2.16 and graphical presentation indicates that the majority (75.15 per cent) of respondents have expressed that they have improved in their income. Whereas 4.44 per cent of respondents has no improvement in their income. The remaining 20.41 per cent have partial improvement in their income.

Political Development:

The political awareness, participation and attitude of the people are some crucial factors and important aspects in the success of the democracy. In India, most of the poor people may not understand the spirit of democracy due to their illiteracy and ignorance. So the effort of NGOs in this context is very much needed to make the poorer sections of the society to become aware of the rights and also to build healthy educated society. It is important to develop political and civil consciousness among the poor people. The political consciousness is key element for development. Knowing the value of the democratic process of administration is very much essential. Though people are illiterates and ignorants, but political awareness is generated with the efforts of Ngos.

In this, it deals with the political development of beneficiaries by understanding various elements of political involvement, and knowledge such as membership in political parties, position as leader. Level of awareness on right to vote, knowledge on the positions of MPs and MLAs , knowledge on the government agencies working for development.

Table 4.2.17: Distribution of Beneficiaries by their Membership in various Political parties

S. No.	*Membership in various Political parties*	*Frequency*	*Percentage*
1.	Congress	405	40.91
2.	Telugu Desham	366	36.97
3.	Praja Rajyam	154	15.55
4.	Other parties	65	6.57
	Total	**990**	**100**

Graph 4.2.17: Distribution of Beneficiaries by their Membership in various Political parties

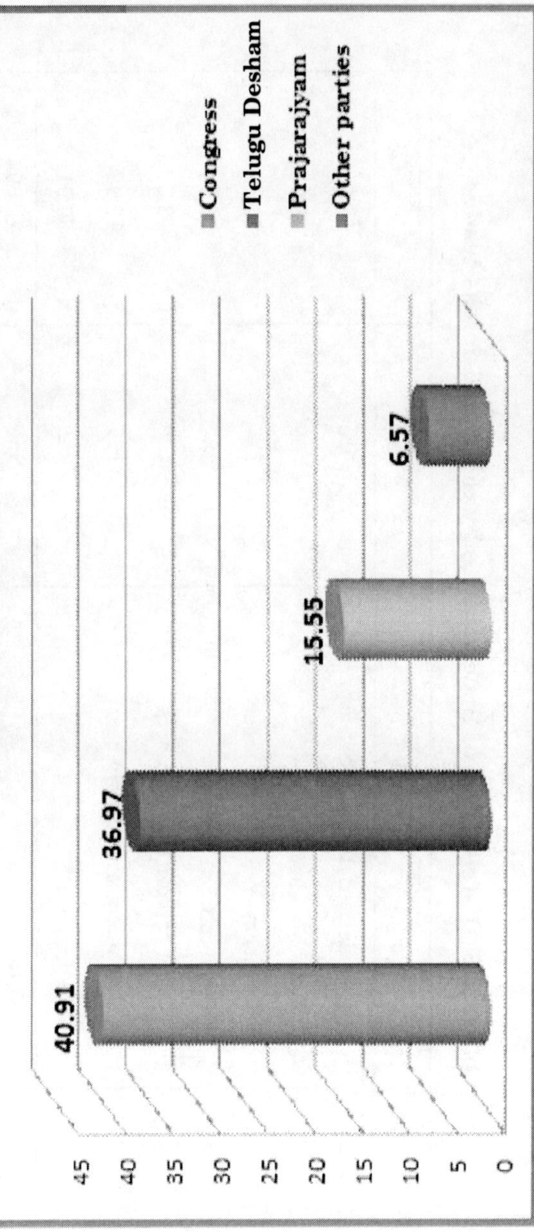

Table 4.2.18: Distribution of Beneficiaries by their position as leader

S. No.	*position as leader*	*Frequency*	*Percentage*
1.	President of the Village (Sarpanch)	15	1.51
2.	Ward Member	59	5.96
3.	Cooperative society member	117	11.82
4.	Leadership in SHG	237	23.94
5.	Other committee members	129	13.03
6.	School committee members	127	12.83
7.	No position	306	30.91
	Total	**990**	**100**

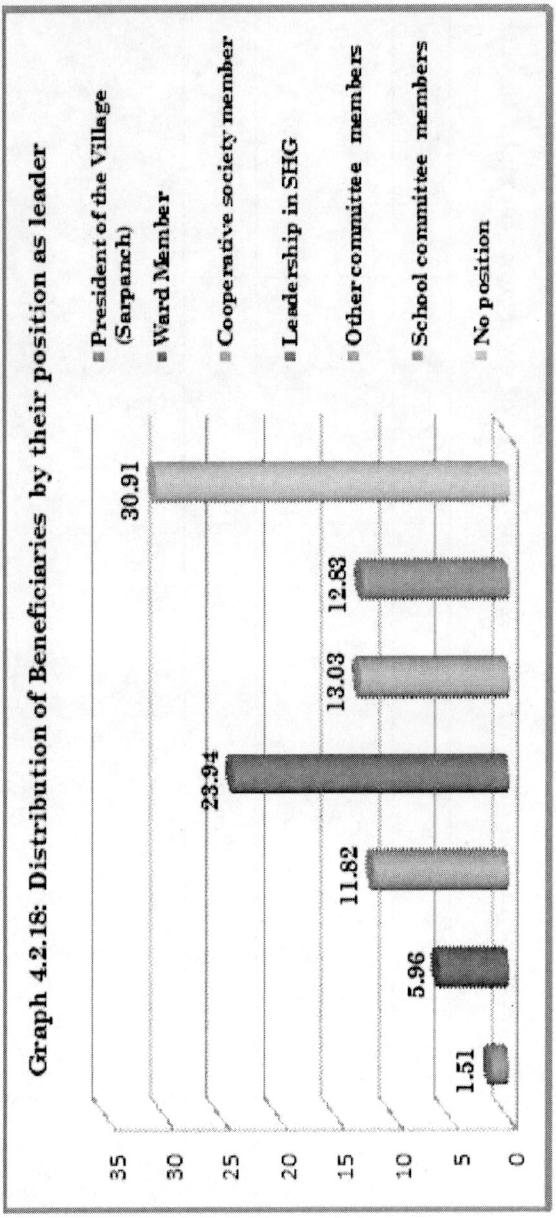

Graph 4.2.18: Distribution of Beneficiaries by their position as leader

Table 4.2.19: Distribution of Beneficiaries by their level of awareness on right to vote

S. No.	*Level of awareness on right to vote*	*Frequency*	*Percentage*
1.	High	974	98.38
2.	Low	16	1.62
	Total	**990**	**100**

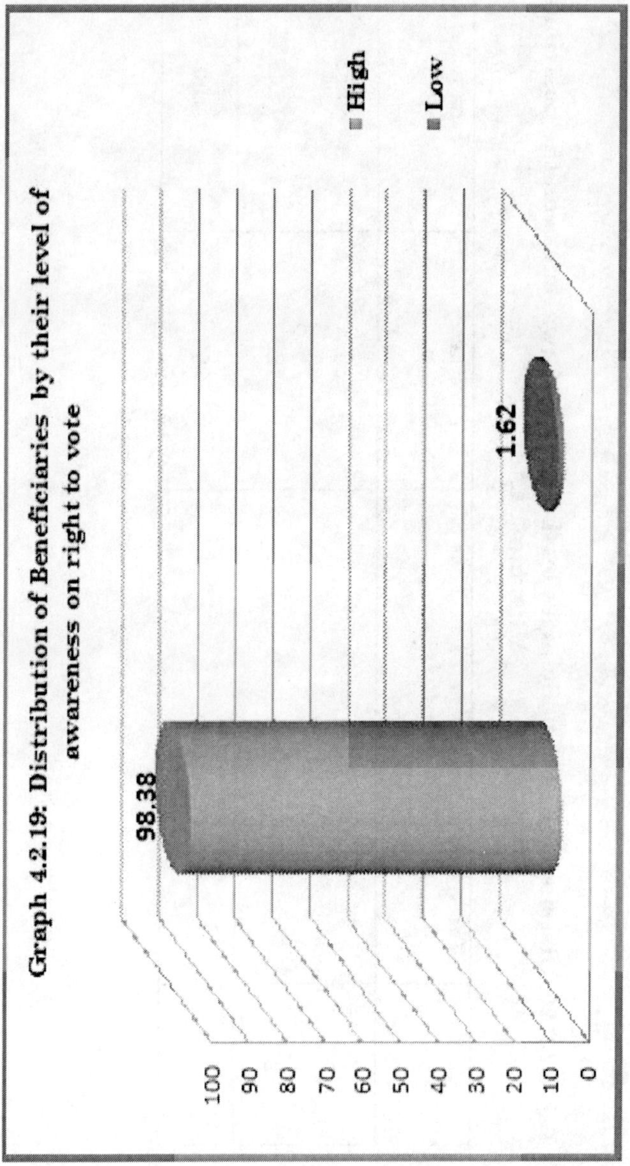

Graph 4.2.19: Distribution of Beneficiaries by their level of awareness on right to vote

Table 4.2.20: Distribution of Beneficiaries by their level of awareness on the positions of MPs and MLAs

S. No.	*The level of awareness on the positions of MPs and MLAs*	*Frequency*	*Percentage*
1.	High	867	87.58
2.	Low	123	12.42
	Total	**990**	**100**

Graph 4.2.21: Distribution of Beneficiaries by their level of awareness on the positions of MPs and MLAs

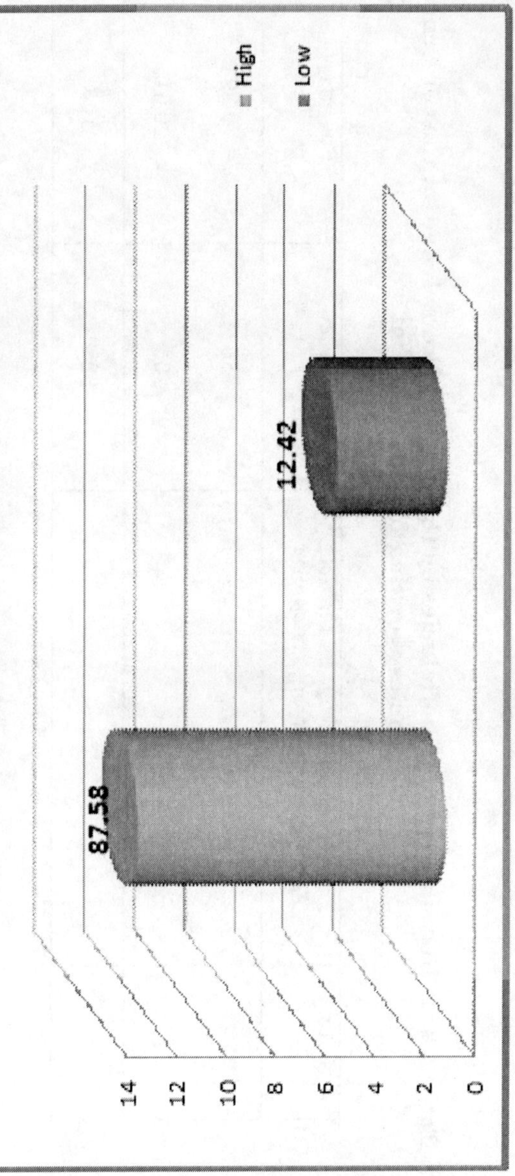

Table 4.2.22: Distribution of Beneficiaries by their level of knowledge on the Government Agencies working for development

S. No.	*The level of knowledge on the Govt. Agencies working for development*	*Frequency*	*Percentage*
1.	High	786	79.39
2.	Low	204	20.61
	Total	**990**	**100**

Graph 4.2.22: Distribution of Beneficiaries by their level of knowledge on the Government Agencies working for development

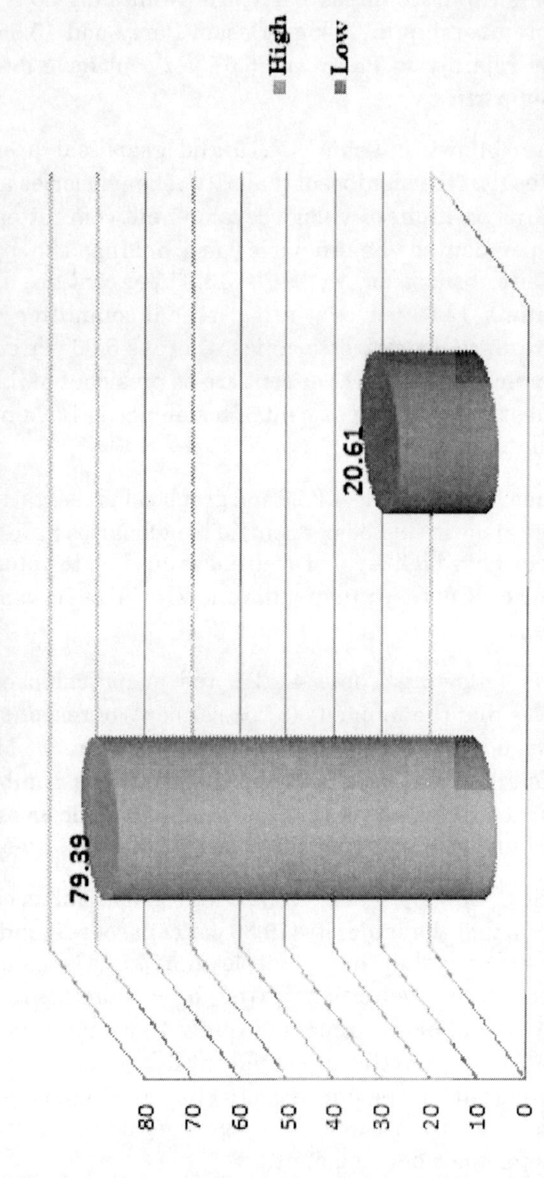

The following Table 4.2.18 and graphical presentation reveals that the majority (40.91 per cent) of respondents have membership in Congress party, the remaining 36.97 per cent have membership in Telugu Desam Party and 15.55 per cent are in Prajarajyam Party and 6.57 per cent have membership in other parties.

The following Table 4.2.19 and graphical presentation indicates that the significant majority of beneficiaries are leaders in various positions of village development committees such as 23.94 per cent of beneficiaries are holding the position of President or secretary in SHG's, 13.03 per cent are in mothers committee, 12.83 per cent are in school committee, 11.82 per cent are in co-operative societies whereas 5.96 per cent are as ward members and 1.51 per cent are as president of the villages. The substantial 30.91 per cent of beneficiaries have no position as leaders.

Thefollowing Table 4.2.20 and graphical presentation reveals that the majority (98.38 per cent) of beneficiaries have expressed that they have high level of awareness on right to vote. Whereas 1.62 per cent of respondents have low level awareness on right to vote.

The following Table 4.2.21 and graphical presentation indicates that the majority (87.58 per cent) of respondents have expressed that they are aware of the positions of Member of Parliament (MPs) and Member of Legislative Assembly (MLAs) in their areas. Whereas 12.42 per cent of beneficiaries have low level of understanding on the positions of MPs and MLAs.

The following Table 4.2.22 and graphical presentation indicates that the majority (79.39 per cent) of respondents have expressed that they have high level of knowledge on various Governmental agencies working for development. Whereas 20.61 per cent of respondents express that they have low level of knowledge on the governmental agencies working for development. It is noted that the significant percent of beneficiaries are aware of the agencies and also availing the grants for their development.

Cultural and Religious Development:

Cultural Traditions and Customs are marked differently in Indian society. The Indian system of caste-ism adhered to by all racial groups belonging to the Hindu religious fold. Lambasted by many as a retrogressive Cultural tradition, this system has also given the Indians a sense of belongingness to a shared way of life. Though caste rigidity was prevalent in the olden times, now it has become flexible to a large extent. Basically a male dominated society, decision making at family and political level is almost single handedly handled by the men. Customs such as Dowry are worsening the process of subjugating women in the society. Oflate, with social awareness about women's vital role in the development of a community or the country, there has been a change in the perception of gender equations in favor of women. Education of women, giving the women a greater say in decision making in the family and the governance are emphasized.

An attempt is made to understand the changes in the cultural practices. The object of NGOs is not only for social and economic development but also change their attitudes, habits, cultural practices of life if they are unscientific and detrimental to their progress in life and to their better living. In this, it deals with religious values and cultural practices of the beneficiaries. To understand this aspect the selected questions related to their religious system and cultural pattern were asked, such as, belief on fate of life, faith on god, living moral life, practice of cultural traits, and belief in superstition.

The following Table 4.2.23 and graphical presentation shows that the majority (50.71 per cent) of beneficiaries have expressed that they changed their belief in fate of life. Whereas 10.60 per cent have belief in fate of life. The remaining 38.69 per cent have partially changed their belief in fate of life. It is noted that the significant percent have changed belief in fate of life into constant effort in the life.

The following Table 4.2.24 and graphical presentation indicates that the majority (87.17 per cent) of beneficiaries have

Table 4.2.23: Distribution of Beneficiaries by their change of belief on fate of life

S. No.	*Change of belief on fate of life*	*Frequency*	*Percentage*
1.	Changed	502	50.71
2.	Partially Changed	383	38.69
3.	Not Changed	105	10.60
	Total	**990**	**100**

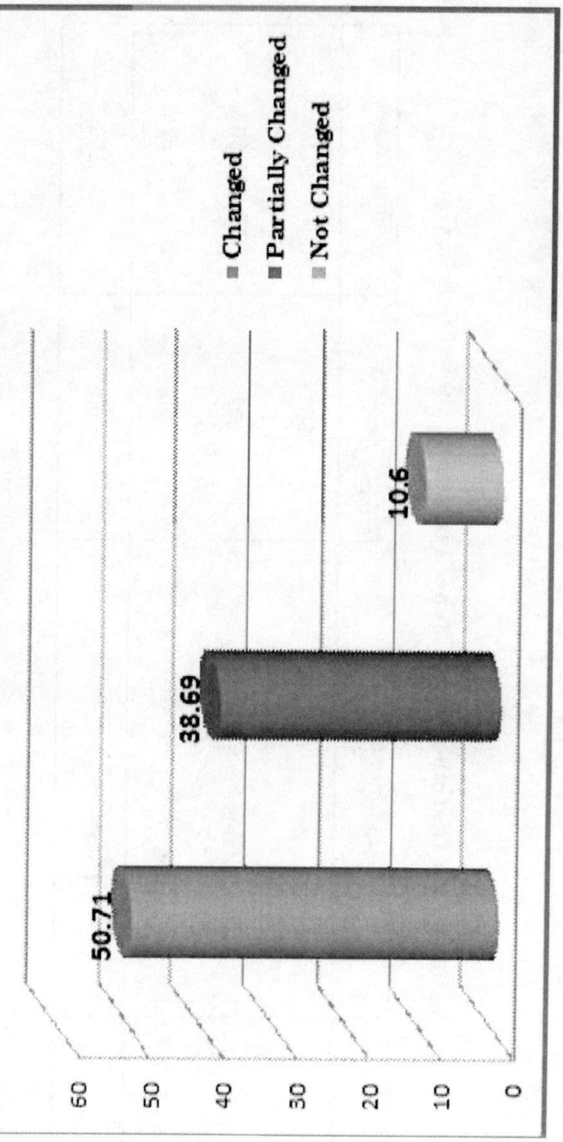

Graph 4.2.23: Distribution of Beneficiaries by their change of belief on fate of life

Table 4.2.24: Distribution of Beneficiaries by their faith in God

S. No.	*Faith in God*	*Frequency*	*Percentage*
1.	Strong	863	87.17
2.	Average	102	10.30
3.	Low	25	2.53
	Total	**990**	**100**

Graph 4.2.24: Distribution of Beneficiaries by their faith in God

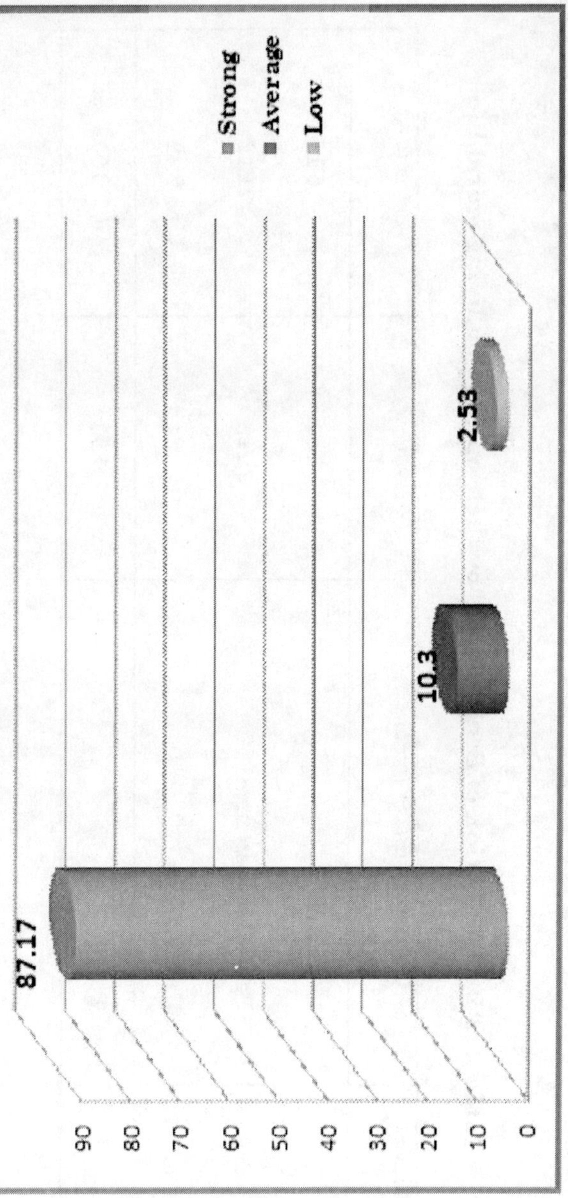

Table 4.2.25: Distribution of Beneficiaries by their opinion on living moral life

S. No.	*Opinion on Living moral Life*	*Frequency*	*Percentage*
1.	Important	754	76.16
2.	Partially important	212	21.42
3.	Un important	24	2.42
	Total	**990**	**100**

Graph 4.2.25: Distribution of Beneficiaries by their opinion on living moral life

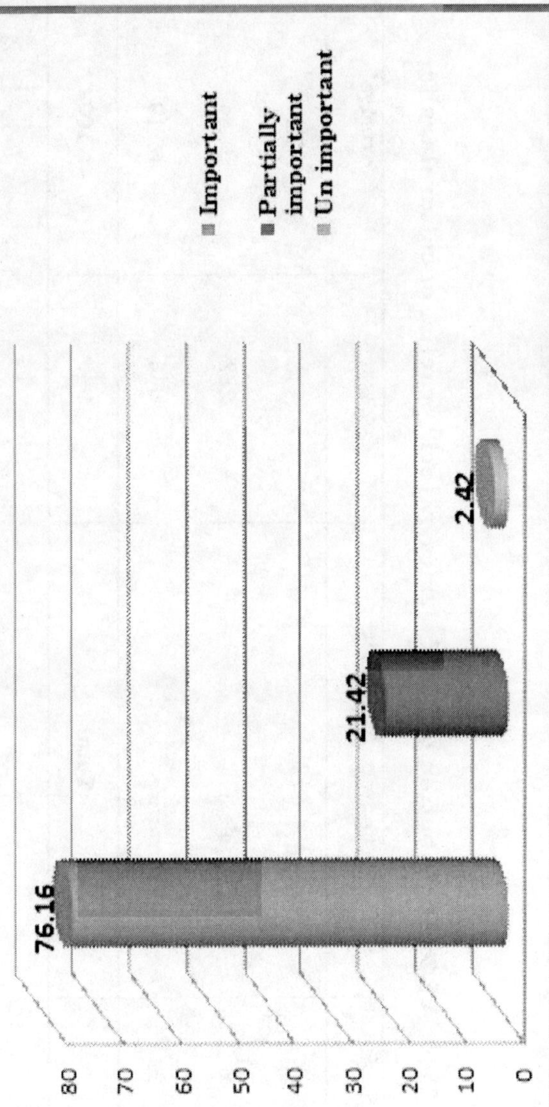

Table 4.2.26: Distribution of Beneficiaries by their practice of cultural traits

S. No.	*Practice of cultural traits*	*Frequency*	*Percentage*
1.	Rigid	73	7.37
2.	Flexible	232	23.44
3.	No practice	685	69.19
	Total	**990**	**100**

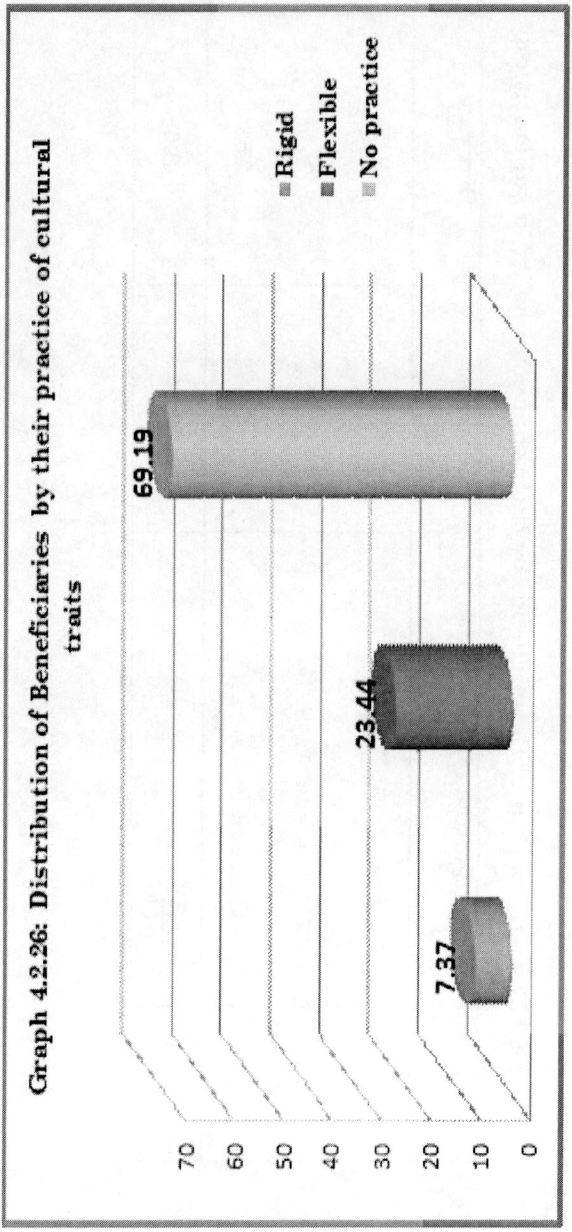

Graph 4.2.26: Distribution of Beneficiaries by their practice of cultural traits

Table 4.2.27: Distribution of Beneficiaries by their change in belief in superstition

S. No.	*Change in belief in superstition*	*Frequency*	*Percentage*
1.	Changed	763	77.07
2.	Partially Changed	202	20.40
3.	Not Changed	25	2.53
	Total	**990**	**100**

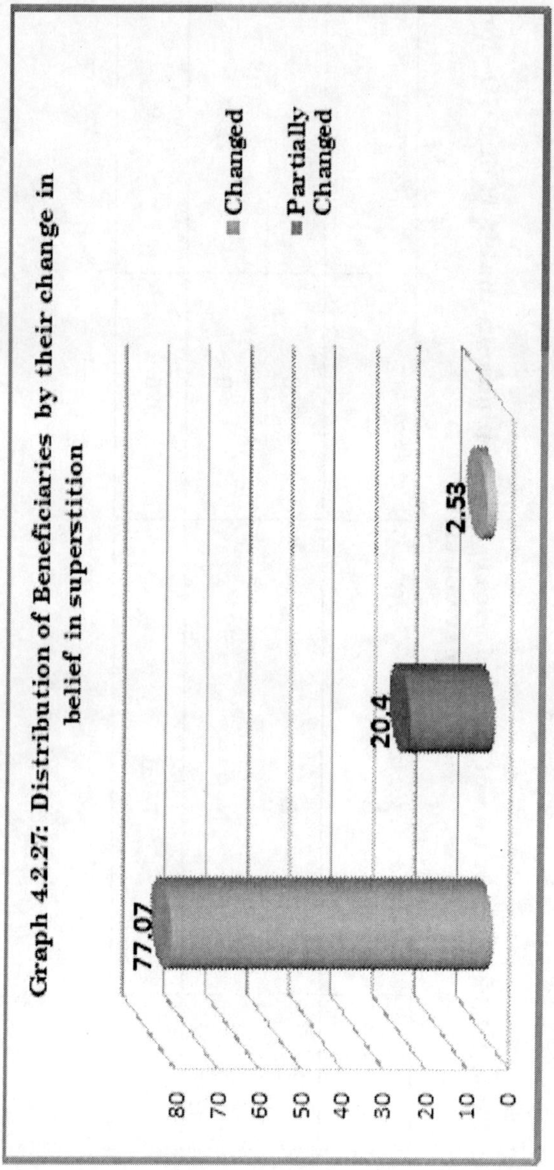

Graph 4.2.27: Distribution of Beneficiaries by their change in belief in superstition

Table 4.2.28: Distribution of Beneficiaries by their opinion in the effort of NGOs for development

S. No.	*Opinion in the effort of NGOs for development*	*Frequency*	*Percentage*
1.	Yes	970	97.98
2.	No	20	2.02
	Total	**990**	**100**

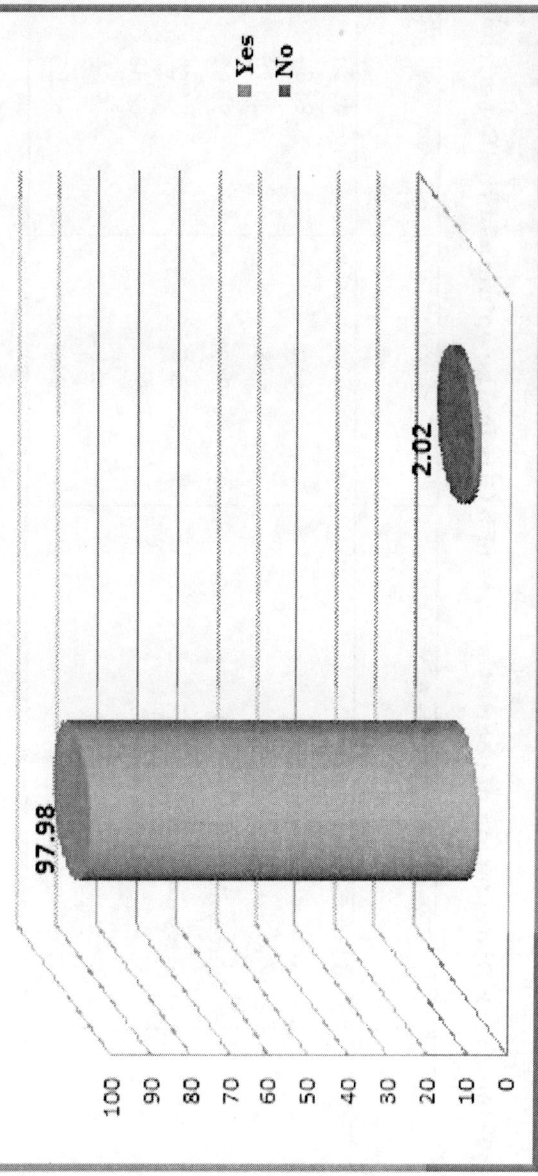

Graph 4.2.28: Distribution of Beneficiaries by their opinion in the effort of NGOs for development

Table 4.2.29: Distribution of characteristics of NGOs by the opinion of the Beneficiaries

S. No.	*Views of Beneficiaries on NGOs*	*Frequency N=990*	*Percentage (%)*
1.	Physical Appearance	656	66.26
2.	Competence	835	84.34
3.	Credibility	953	96.26
4.	Accessibility	950	95.96
5.	Responsiveness	680	68.69
6.	Support and Security	867	87.58
7.	Sensitivity	889	89.80
8.	Communication	646	65.25

Graph 4.2.29: Distribution of characteristics of NGOs by the opinion of the Beneficiaries

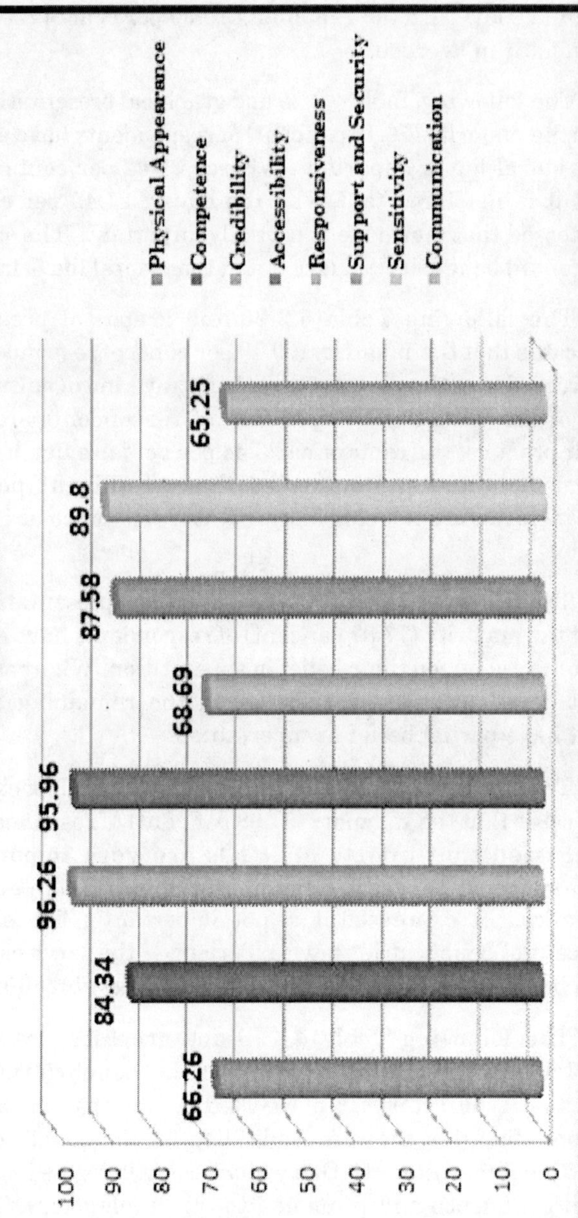

expressed that they have strong faith in God. Whereas 2.53 per cent have low faith the remaining 10.30 per cent of respondents have faith in average.

The following Table 4.2.25 and graphical presentation shows that the majority (76.16 per cent) of respondents have expressed that moral life is important. Whereas 2.42 per cent expressed that it is not important. The remaining 21.42 per cent have expressed that moral life is partially important. The significant percent of beneficiaries have noted that moral life is important.

The following Table 4.2.26 and graphical presentation indicates that the majority (69.19 per cent) of respondents have expressed that they are not practising any kind of cultural traits or norms. Whereas 7.37 per cent of respondents are rigid in their practice, the remaining 23.44 per cent are flexible in their cultural matters. It is noted that significant percent of beneficiaries are not considering cultural practice as important factor.

The following Table 4.2.27 and graphical presentation shows that the majority (77.07 per cent) of respondents have expressed that they changed their belief in superstition. Whereas 2.53 per cent have not changed their belief, the remaining 20.40 per cent have partial belief in superstition.

The following Table 4.2.28 and graphical presentation indicates that the majority (97.98 per cent) of respondents have expressed that efforts of NGOs are very important for development. Whereas negligible number (2.02 per cent) of beneficiaries expressed it is not important. The significant percent of beneficiaries have experienced the services of NGOs and believed on their constant efforts for development.

The following Table 4.2.29 and graphical presentation explains more on the opinions of the beneficiaries on the functional characteristics of NGOs. The majority (96.26 per cent) of beneficiaries viewed credibility as the most important functional character of NGOs which strengthens the beneficiaries with confidence and promotes social development. The most significant percent 95.96 per cent of beneficiaries have expressed their opinion that accessibility is also important functional character of NGOs. It is noted that 89.80 per cent of beneficiaries viewed sensitivity as the deserved characters of NGO which promotes better understanding of the real socio-economic condition of the people. It is revealed that 87.58 per cent of beneficiaries have expressed that support and security is also a needed character of NGO where as 65.25 per cent of beneficiaries viewed that communication is also a functional character of NGOs. The remaining 84.34 per cent expressed on competence, 68.69 per cent viewed on responsiveness and 66.26 per cent viewed on physical appearance. It is noted that the majority that is more than 60 per cent of beneficiaries viewed that all functional characters are important for NGOs for better functioning towards social development.

Chapter - V

Summary, Suggestions and Conclusions

5

Summary, Suggestions and Conclusions

In this chapter, summary, suggestions and certain valid conclusions are extracted on the basis of objectively quantified results and some are presente d as follows. The major objective of the study is to find out the role of NGO's in Social contribution for development. The present study helped to understand the actual role-played and various methods employed in the process of Social contribution for development.

The NGO's under study have taken enormous efforts and used various methods and development schemes. Based on the results of the present study, it is clear that the efforts of the NGOs helped a lot in promoting, strengthening, and stabilizing the various development schemes. The NGOs under study revealed that they had clear-cut objectives for Social development in mind before starting the process. Their objectives for Social development were to create equalities among the various communities, to promote standard of living, economical Improvement, to strengthen the unity among the people, to make them responsible, to remove inequality among the men and women, to bring out their potential skill, leadership development among the women, to increase their contribution in successful implementation of the schemes, to identify their needs and problems, to understanding the spirits of the people, awareness generation and to remove dependency, skill and capacity development, to make them realize their potentials, to reduce bureaucracy, to promote Spirit of Voluntarism .The views of the beneficiaries was taken into consideration for the real output of the efforts of the NGOs. in Vizianagaram.

Summary

The research study focused on designation of functionaries working in NGOs. It is found that majority (30 per cent) of functionaries are project Managers followed by 25 per cent of functionaries are chief secretaries, whereas 19 per cent are programme coordinators. It is noted that the key functionaries are Project Managers and Chief Secretaries.

The research study indicated on the work experience of functionaries in NGOs. It is noted that majority (75 per cent) of functionaries have 0 to 3 years of work experience, whereas 9 per cent of functionaries have 6 years and above experience. It is noted that most of the functionaries have less work experience as there is frequent mobility of functionaries

The research study focused on the task assigned to functionaries. It is found that majority (34 per cent) of functionaries are assigned with income generated tasks and 26 per cent are assigned with health related issues. Most of the NGOs are working for economic development as well as promotion of good health.

The research study focused on the year of establishment of NGOs. It is noted that majority (30 per cent) of NGOs are established during 2001-2005. Whereas 22 per cent of NGOs are established during 1983-1988. Most of the NGOs are working for 5 and above years.

The research study reveals the number of employees engaged in NGOs. It is noted that majority (53 per cent) of NGOs are functioning with less than 15 employees. Whereas 18 per cent of NGOs having more than 30 employees.

The research study indicated on the coverage of Revenue Mandals in Vizianagaram District by the NGOs. It is noted that the majority (48 per cent) of NGOs are working between 5-10 mandals, whereas 32 per cent of NGOs are working in less than 5 mandals. Regarding the coverage of mandals it is noted that required contribution is done by the NGOs in their respective operational areas.

The research study indicates on the focused area of work done by the NGOs. It is noted that majority (31 per cent) of NGOs focused on economic development followed by 30 per cent are at education. It is clear that most of the operational areas are backward areas. The people of the area are below poverty line, where education and economic development activities are deserved.

The research study reveals the major funding agencies from where the NGOs are receiving grants for development. It is noted that the majority (45 per cent) of NGOs are receiving funds from State Government followed by 20 per cent are from Central Government. Only 10 per cent of funds received from International agencies.

The research study revels the annual budgets of NGOs. It is noted that majority (53 per cent) of NGOs are having their annual budget between 5-10 lakhs followed by 33 per cent are receiving between 11-15 lakhs.

The research study focuses on the type of social workers engaged in NGOs. It is focused that the majority (70 per cent) of employees are untrained social workers, whereas 30 per cent of social workers are trained. It is opinined the untrained social workers may not work with professional skills and capacities.

The research study reveals on the availability of Website of NGOs. It is noted that majority (94 per cent) of NGOs have no website, whereas 6 per cent of NGOs have their own websites. It is also noted that the majority of NGOs have no good networking connections with outside the world.

The research study revels the location of head office of NGOs. It is noted that majority (68 per cent) of NGOs have located their head office at operational area. The remaining 32 per cent are at district head quarters. It is clear that most of the NGOs are accessible to the people. Accessibility is the most important character of the NGOs.

The research study focuses on the opinions of functionaries of NGOs on their key achievements. It is noted that majority (13 per cent) of functionaries viewed economic sustainability is their key achievement followed by 10 per cent capacity building and 10 per cent awareness in all aspects . The remaining 9 per cent Improving Literacy rate ,9 per cent participation in development activities ,8 per cent improved health conditions ,8 per cent women empowerment ,8 per cent livestock improvement ,8 per cent advocacy, 6 per centSelf Efficacy , 6 per centcultural change and 5 per cent environmental development as the key achievements. All the key achievements of NGOs proved their contribution towards development..

The research study focuses on the regular monitoring and supervision systems of NGOs. It is noted that the majority (75 per cent) of NGOs are having regular monitoring and supervision in which 31 per cent are conducting internal monitoring and 27 per cent are conducting external monitoring, whereas 18 per cent are conducting both internal and external monitoring and supervision. It is also noted that 33 per cent of NGOs are conducting monitoring and supervision by monthly and 31 per cent are conducting annual monitoring and supervision.

The research study reveals the Interactive networking with other agencies by NGOs. It is noted that majority (60 per cent) are having network with state government, whereas 10 per cent have with Central government, the remaining 15 per cent are having with academic institutions.

The research study focused on the socio-economic profile of the beneficiaries. It is noted that majority (46.87 per cent) of beneficiaries are between the age group of 18-28. Most of the beneficiaries are young and energetic. Most of (53.13 per cent) the beneficiaries belong to nuclear families whereas 46.87 per cent are in joint families. The majority (53.43 per cent) of beneficiaries belong to scheduled caste. The beneficiaries who belong to backward caste and scheduled caste are poor and having low social status. The majority (63.54 per cent) of beneficiaries belongs to Hindu religion, whereas 23.13 per cent are Christians.

Most of (46.67 per cent) the beneficiaries are illiterates and 35.25 per cent have primary education. It is noted that majority (41.82 per cent) of beneficiaries are having income between Rs 1001 to Rs 2000, whereas 9.29 per cent are having income of Rs 3000 and above per month.

The research study focused on the opinion of the Beneficiaries on their development of life. The majority (64.24 per cent) of beneficiaries expressed that they have partially developed in all aspects in their life and 9.59 per cent expressed that they have low development and 26.17 per cent expressed that they developed in all aspects of life.

The research study reveals on the opinion of beneficiaries on various aspects of development. The majority (92.83 per cent) have expressed that they have developed in economic position in their life and 83.54 per cent of beneficiaries found some change in social aspect of development and 65.56 per cent are on political development and 50.20 per cent are in cultural and religious development. It is clear that most of the beneficiaries are financially improved, socially empowered and political activated.

The research focused on the infrastructural development as viewed by the Beneficiaries. The majority (89.49 per cent) of beneficiaries expressed that there is infrastructural development and 10.51 per cent have mentioned that there is no infrastructural development. Infrastructure like housing, transportation, drainage system, schools, primary health centres, community halls etc.

The research study focused on the practice of social evils by the beneficiaries. The majority (87.27 per cent) have expressed that they are not practising any kind of social evils and 10.73 per cent of beneficiaries are under practice of social evils, such as child marriages, sati, widow remarriages, untouchability etc., It is noted that the efforts of NGOs in creating awareness on social evils through rally programs and constant training programs has resulted better changes in the life style of the people.

The research study reveals the opinion of the beneficiaries on the improvement of education. The majority (56.26 per cent) have expressed that there is improvement in education and 32.42 per cent have expressed that there is partial improvement and 11.82 per cent have expressed that there is no improvement in education. It is noted that improvement in education is the key element for development. Most of the NGOs conducted literacy camps , non formal education and adult education programmes for better improvement in education. It is also noted that more than 50 per cent have expressed that there is improvement in their education through which they benefited and improved in their life.

The research study focused on the improvement of the status of women. The majority (54.24 per cent) of beneficiaries expressed that there is a significant improvement on the status of women and 34.55 per cent have expressed that there is a partial improvement in status of women. It is noted that the status of women is very much improved because of their education, participation and decision making as well as economic independence and self reliance. The efforts of NGOs in bringing out drastic changes in the life styles of women has produced better results.

The research study indicates the self image of the beneficiaries. The majority (65.15 per cent) of beneficiaries expressed that they gained self image and 24.55 per cent expressed that their self image is partially improved. It is noted that self image promoted self respect and dignity to the beneficiaries because of their development in social, economic and political aspects.

The research study focused on the level of awareness on various laws related to life for better standards of living. The majority (64.04 per cent) have expressed that they are aware of the laws and 23.54 per cent have expressed that they have average knowledge on laws. The laws related to life such as dowry prohibition act, information act, domestic violence act and child labour act, minimum wages act and so on. Being aware of laws they became more dynamic and participative in all activities. It also helps them to overcome certain problems in life and thus helps for better living.

The research study reveals on the awareness of beneficiaries on health facilities. The majority (89.49 per cent) of beneficiaries are availing of all health facilities provided by the central and state governments. It is noted that the NGOs provided necessary information on health schemes and facilities such as Arogyasri, 104, 108, Mobile health services and so on.

The research study focused on the savings of the beneficiaries in the Banks. The majority (90.81 per cent) of beneficiaries have their savings in the bank. It is noted that significant number of beneficiaries are having knowledge on bank transactions. This knowledge on bank transaction was given by the NGOs through training in workshops which is a process of capacity building towards financial independence.

The research study revealed on the knowledge of beneficiaries in availing bank loans. The majority (90.61 per cent) of beneficiaries are availing bank loans. It is noted that significant number of beneficiaries are financially improved by savings in the bank .It helped them to get loans from the Banks and to overcome from the problem of paying high interests for the money given by money lenders.

The research study focused on the improvement of assets and livestock of the beneficiaries. The majority (69.60 per cent) have partially improved and 23.84 per cent beneficiaries are very much improved in their assets and livestock. This indicates their economic development.

The research study focused on the present position of beneficiaries as self reliant. The majority (88.38 per cent) of beneficiaries are self reliant and 11.60 per cent are not self reliant. It is noted that significant number of respondents have gained the position of self reliance.

The research study focused on the opinion of the beneficiaries on experience in financial exploitation. The majority (65.25 per cent) have not experienced any financial exploitation. The negligible number (4.24 per cent) are still under the clutches of financial exploitation. It is found that 30.51 per cent of beneficiaries are experiencing financial exploitation at average level. It is evident that significant number of respondents have gained financial stability and freedom.

The research study focused on improvement of level of income of the beneficiaries. The majority (75.15 per cent) have improved their income. The negligible number (4.4 per cent) are not improved their income. It is noted that 20.41 per cent have partially improved their income. It is noted that most of the beneficiaries have improved their income and living standard of life because of the efforts of NGOs towards the economic development.

The research study reveals on the membership in various political parties by the beneficiaries to understand more about the political development. The majority (40.91 per cent) have taken membership in Congress party and 36.97 per centhave taken membership in Telugu Desam. Majority of respondents have taken membership in National and Regional parties. Almost all the beneficiaries have membership in one or the other Political party.

The research study focused on the beneficiarie's position as leader . Most of the beneficiaries are leaders in cooperative societies and SHGs ,school committees as well as other committees . It is noted that 5.96 per cent of beneficiaries are elected as ward members and 1.51 per cent of beneficiaries are elected as the president of the village.

The research study focused on the level of awareness of the beneficiaries on right to vote. The majority (98.38 per cent) have high level of awareness from right to vote. The negligible number (1.62 per cent) have low level of awareness. It is noted that beneficiaries are having very good awareness on political system such as active participation in election system and knowledge on democratic principles.

The research study reveals on the level of awareness of beneficiaries on the position of M.Ps and MLAs). The majority (95.56 per cent) have high level of awareness on position of MPs and MLAs. The negligible number (4.44 per cent) are having low level of awareness. It is noted that most of the beneficiaries are aware of the constitutional pattern of administration and the position of leaders.

The research study focused on the level of knowledge of the beneficiaries on government agencies working for development. The majority (79.39 per cent) have high level of knowledge on various government agencies working for development such as CAPART, NABARD, CSWB, ICDS, DRDA. It is noted that significant number of beneficiaries are availing the agencies and also availing grants for their development.

The research study focused the change of belief system of beneficiaries on fate of life. The majority (50.71 per cent) have changed their belief system in fate of life and 38.69 per cent have partially changed. It is noted that the significant number of beneficiaries are culturally changed in their practice and belief.

The research study focused on the beneficiaries' faith in god. The majority (87.17 per cent) are having strong faith in god. It is noted that all the beneficiaries have faith in god. This indicates the religious faith and spirituality of the beneficiaries

The research study focused on the opinion of the beneficiaries on living moral life. The majority (76.16 per cent) have expressed that living moral life is important only 2.42 per cent have expressed that it is unimportant. It is noted that majority of beneficiaries expressed that living moral life is very important. This indicates that they are standing for strong moral life which indicates their religious development.

The research study focused on the practice of cultural traits. The majority (69.19 per cent) are not practising any cultural traits and 23.44 per cent are flexible in their practice. It is noted that most of the beneficiaries are culturally changed by avoiding some unimportant cultural norms and customs which are blocking the development of the people.

The research study focused on the change at belief in superstition of beneficiaries . The majority (77.07 per cent) of beneficiaries expressed that they changed their belief in superstation and 20.40 per cent are partially changed. Belief in superstition indicates that they are living in the primitive stage. It is evident that the most of the beneficiaries are changed their attitude and belief towards superstition.

The research study focused on the opinion of the beneficiaries towards the efforts of NGOs for development. The majority (97.98 per cent) have expressed that the efforts of the NGOs are very important for development. It is noted that the development has taken place only through the efforts of NGOs.

The research study focused on the opinion of the beneficiaries on various functional characteristics of NGOs such as physical appearance, competence, credibility, accessibility, responsiveness, support and security, sensitivity and communication. It is noted that above 50 per cent of beneficiaries viewed that all the functional characteristics are important, credibility and accessibility are more important.

The research study revealed that the NGOs used the combination of various methods under Extension methods and activities, educational methods and activities, social methods and activities, motivational methods and activities.

Under the Extension methods, the NGOs have used various methods such as film show, street play, social drama through songs, regular meetings, door to door visits and direct contacts, Group and mass contacts and meetings, stay and living in the villages and interacting at nights, in order to organize the people in the process of Social Interaction for development.

Under the Educational Methods, the NGOs have used various methods such as exposure visits, presentation of successful Case Studies, film shows, pictorial presentation, live demonstration, charts reflecting social issues, Non – Formal Education, News reading in the groups in order to organize the people in the process of Social Interaction

Under the Social Methods, the NGOs have employed and used various methods such as mingling with the people, meeting during the social gatherings, participatory learning and discussions, social games and sports, hearing their problems, addressing the Grama Sabha, relationship building, understanding their problems and offering solution, conducting sports for women and children, appreciations during the mass gatherings, competitions and distribution of gifts for school children, enrollment drive during school beginning, motivation methods and activities, providing subsidy, integrating government subsidy schemes, incentives in the form of food materials, distribution of awards and rewards, inculcating saving habits, promoting group concepts, linking with government schemes etc.

Suggestions

It is suggested to the NGOs to take initiatives in appointing women as a functionary and it is recommended to use the term facilitator in the designations.

It is suggested that the high positions in the NGOs should be given to the experienced employees so that the guidance and management will be positive.

It is recommended to the NGOs to consider field based realities and need of the beneficiary while assigning the task to the functionaries.

It is advised to the functionaries of NGOs to realize that development consists of various other aspects of life, economic development is one among them.

It is suggested to the NGOs to recruit qualified, trained and experienced social workers to render the quality services .

It is advised to the NGOs to work in the limited mandals and extend services to the maximum number of villages.

It is suggested to focus more on education as well as income generating schemes and also on cultural and religious aspects.

It is advised to the NGOs to receive grants from Central Government, International agency and multi-national companies, as these companies are focusing on corporate social responsibility.

It is suggested to the NGOs to avail more funds from the International Agencies and multinational companies in the name of backwardness and under development of the District.

It is suggested to the NGOs to recruit more professionally trained social workers to provide quality services to the beneficiaries. So that they can utilize their professional skills and capacities.

It is advised to the NGOs to create their own website with all their activities and update information and this provides them wider chances to connect with International NGOs where they can contact for better projects.

It is suggested to NGOs to have head office in the Head Quarters of the district so that there will be better contacts and information with the Government agencies at the same time have sub- office in the operational area which is equally important.

It is advised to the NGOs to focus on all the activities for overall development of the beneficiaries.

It is advised to the NGOs to have regular monitoring in supervision at least once in a month preferably with professionals for better progress.

It is advised to the NGOs to develop interaction and networking system with academic institutions to update their knowledge on the field of development. It is also suggested to maintain interaction not only with the donor agency but also with other agencies.

It is advised to the NGOs to focus more on the various elements of social development such as education, health, infrastructural development, status of women improving self image to understand the development of the beneficiaries in social conditions.

It is suggested to create awareness on various laws related to life for better standards of living of the beneficiaries through continuous and constant training programs.

It is suggested to NGOs to take necessary measures to bring out the beneficiaries out of financial exploitation by providing economic support.

It is advised to the NGOs to promote self reliance system to all the beneficiaries to come out of the clutches of money lenders.

It is suggested to the NGOs to promote economic development by encouraging the beneficiaries for savings and in availing bank loans and initiating small business centers and by improving their assets and livestock.

It is suggested to the NGOs to focus on the political development of the beneficiaries by promoting awareness on democratic values and principles, and also by leadership and decision making power.

It is suggested to the NGOs to focus not only on the social and economic development of the beneficiaries but also cultural and religious aspects.

It is advised to the NGOs to develop credibility and accessibility as important characters which are viewed by the beneficiaries. It is important to take the views of the beneficiaries into consideration.

It is suggested to provide proper understanding on the importance of designations of the functionaries to play their responsible roles.

It is suggested that the functionaries should be refreshed with latest developments and updated information for better growth in the development aspects of NGOs.

It is suggested to design and deliver intensive training to functionaries for updating their knowledge, skills and attitude from time to time considering their age, education and experiences.

It is suggested that work assignments of the functionaries should have rotation and innovations in the NGO.

It is recommended that Professional Skills of the functionaries constitute core areas when organizational interventions are essential. Skills in helping people need to be updated from time to time. Multi-skilling has been inevitable and need to be introduced in the overall functioning of the NGOs. Functionaries should be provided with job rotation so that they can enhance their skill related to different fields so as to make them multi-skilled

It is suggested that both NGO's and functionaries should periodically assess their perception of values that exist and their compatibility with the objectives, missions and mission of the NGO.

It is suggested that various approaches and strategies should be adopted to improve the quality of life such as quality circles, teamwork, autonomous group working, flex timing. self management and direct participative intervention .

It is suggested that the physical locations and conditions of the NGO's are of prime significance for the functionaries as well for beneficiaries. The location, transport facilities, geographical area, infrastructures, the uses of modern appliances etc are very crucial in delivering services.

It is suggested to enhance the level of job involvement of the functionaries from policy formation stage to implementations and evaluation stage of the NGOs. The job/task assigned to the employees should be interesting, and not of repetitive nature, which calls for creativity on the part of the functionaries and which ensures their greater involvement.

It is suggested that Communication and Access to information determines the effectiveness of the functionaries. NGO needs to improve these techniques by encouraging newer experiments, promotion of working with cross-functional, educative and informative workshops, functional and behavioural training etc. Functionaries of the NGO's need to give and take feedback from their beneficiaries on regular basis which can help, improve their performance level.

It is suggested that NGO's should work to increase the motivational level of their functionaries allowing creativity and empowering them to take initiatives in order to find out better ways of performing their respective tasks.

It is recommended that the job-task assigned to the functionaries should be such that it provides opportunities to use the human potentials to the optimum level and to develop the human capacities.

It is suggested that decentralization and empowerment should take place from apex authorities of NGO which will lead to getting faster result and to speed up the decision making process. The traditional system of performance review should be re-Looked by management as well as functionaries of the NGOs.

It is suggested that NGOs need to work on mobilizing resources to raise their level of infrastructure to the optimum level to deliver effective services.

It is recommended that the beneficiary need to be more participative involved and more expecting in terms of quality and satisfaction from the services delivered by the NGOs.

It is recommended that a culture of learning is required to be consciously promoted in the NGO's. The beneficiaries of the NGO's will greatly benefit through building and upgrading their knowledge on development and empowerment and other related issues on regular basis through the means of reading, presentations, attending workshops and training programmes .

It is suggested to strengthen a strong networking amongst NGOs working in the fields for greater effectiveness of their performance and their contribution for development

It is recommended that the impressive methods employed by the NGOs can be used elsewhere while they initiate social development process instead of experimenting new methods.

It is recommended that the National and regional level seminars, workshops can be organized to sensitize and build capacity among the NGOs on various issues pertaining to the Social development.

It is recommended that larger level of documentation on very good experiments, experiences, and achievements made by the NGOs, and other developmental organisations on Social development can be made, in order to make this utility wider.

It is recommended that a similar study can be conducted with more NGOs covering more districts to compare the geographical differences on the impact of Social development.

It is recommended that the various methods used by NGOs can be replicated elsewhere to the possible extent for making successful implementation of all developmental programmes in the future.

It is recommended to promote beneficiary's action for participatory democracy and development by supporting collective action for greater accountability.

It is recommended that activity involves a range of non state actors for an outward looking multilateralism that reinforces beneficiary engagement and human development for transformation.

It is recommended that to improve and expand social services including provision for education as well as improvement of physical infrastructure such as roads, electricity water supply and sanitation leading to change in the quality of life.

It is suggested to diversify economic activities and employment opportunities.

It is suggested to redesign and promote NGOs to meet the resources requirements for education including directing resources to improve quality and to overcome disparities.

It is recommended to strengthen of national poverty reduction strategies, including equitable allocation of budgets, and greater accountability and participation of NGOs.

It is recommended to reinforce action oriented programs to meet the felt needs of disadvantaged groups such as children with special needs, migrants, minorities and the rural/urban poor.

It is recommended to recognize that ICTs are only a means and not an end in themselves, their application in all fields of development, especially to reach the unreached and provide for acquisition of additional skills, for better standard of life.

Conclusions

Now there is a wide recognition of the growing global importance of non-governmental actors, and it has emerged as a theoretically exciting and policy relevant field of the social sciences. Research on NGOs is relevant to a very wide range key of social science themes. The efforts of NGOs at local, national and global levels are aiming at poverty reduction and social inclusion, equality and international solidarity. Most of the literature on NGOs deals with their history and activities. No study has ever tried to address the question of assessing their performance and contribution for the social development. The present study, therefore, attempts to study the NGOs that work at the grassroots level with non-profit motive. The analysis of their performance and contribution is necessary to ensure their effective role in the society. The market and state need to play enabling role for the NGOs, especially in terms of finances and legal framework and by involving community at large through adopting participatory method of development. NGOs are the 'social capital' of the society and there is a need to build and sustain the positive 'social capital', which could help in socio-economic development of people. In the present study, the effectiveness is also subject to the beneficiaries perception and their intra-household environs. Hence it is necessary to emphasize that these factors have an impact NGOs' functioning.

The NGOs by their very nature are diverse in structure, organization, nature of activities and purpose and hence their performance criteria would differ in emphasis and content, nonetheless the methodological issues discussed in the research study would help to assess the potentials of NGOs in achieving 'social development'.

The contribution of the NGOs to the domains of social welfare, development, income-generating enterprises, empowerment, and concentisation (the, process whereby people are made aware of their conditions, rights, and expectations) was notable. Even though the work of NGOs in the fields was carried out at the micro levels, in the end it has borne fruits and made a significant impact. It is widely recognized that they have been quite effective in their limited areas of operation.

The roles NGOs perform today are numerous: They are advocates, educators, catalysts, monitors, whistle blowers, mediators, lobbyists, activists, animators, protectors of human rights, concentisation, animators, and conciliators. Notable is the fact that these roles are never played in an affable climate in India.

Certain attempts to formulate a code of conduct for voluntary agencies gained attention. The government, with the support of some prominent NGO leaders, tried to set up an independent National Council that was supposed to monitor the activities of the NGO sector. Amidst stiff opposition from a strong section of the society, the idea was finally dropped. The code of ethics must be formulated by the voluntary organizations themselves.

The importance of NGOs in achieving social development through micro-finance, capacity building and self-reliance is increased. NGOs through the micro-finance help members of community to access jobs, income-generation and improve economic situation. And then they would become empowered economically. On the other hand, NGOs develop the capacities of community such as skills, abilities, knowledge, assets and motivates the community to participate in the project to improve the quality of their lives. NGOs act as capacity builders that help the community to achieve the empowerment particularly individual empowerment. The process involves capacity building, where people get involved in human capital training, transferring of authority from donor to recipient and receive supports from beneficiaries. When people become fully empowered, they are able to contribute towards development. Capacity building and empowerment through trainings, workshops are the best means to achieve the development in all aspects of life . Therefore, NGOs through some programs and functions, such as microfinance, capacity building and self reliance help community to be empowered, and finally contribute towards social development.

Appendix

Appendix

SECTION-I

Questionnaire for the functionaries of non-governmental organisations (ngos) in the vizianagaram – district, andhra pradesh.

- **PROFILE OF RESPONDENT CONTACTED**

1. Name of the Respondent: ______________________________
2. Current Designation in the NGO–

   (a) Chief Coordinator (b) Chief Secretary

   (c) Project Director (d) Project Manager

   (e) Project Coordinator

I. Organisational Profile:

   1. Name of the Organisation;
   2. Year of Establishment;
   3. Year of Registration under Society's Act;
   4. No. of Employees in the Organisation and
   5. Coverage Area:
      - Name of Districts:
      - No. of mandals:

6. Focus Areas:
   - Education
   - Health
   - Environment
   - Human Rights
   - Economy
   - Any Other
7. Major Funding Agencies: (Specify)
   - State Government
   - Central Government
   - Both State and Central Governments
   - International Organisations (NGOs)
   - Multinational Companies
8. Annual Budget for the programs:
   - 5 - 10 Lakhs
   - 11 – 15 Lakhs
   - 16 – 20 Lakhs
   - 20 and above
9. Number of Employees:

   Trained Social Worker Untrained Social Worker

   ____

   ______________________________ :

   ____

   ____

10. Website Address: (If available)

11. Vision and Mission of the Organisation:

____

____

____

____

II. ORGANISATIONAL AND OPERATIONAL DETAILS

Please provide details on the location of headquarter, number of branch/field offices of the NGO at time of inception and at present.

Details	*Currently*
(i) Location of Headquarter	(Specify location) : ________________
(ii) Details of Branch Offices (offices with presence of professionals and control over field operations)	
• Within the State being covered for the study	__________Nos.
• Within Country (excluding state being covered under study)	__________Nos.
(iii) Total No. of Field Offices (Branches with field operations should be reporting to the branch/head office)	
• Within State being covered for the study	__________Nos.
• Within Country (excluding state being covered under study)	__________Nos.
(iv) Whether any international operations exist	1. Yes 2. No

III. DETAILS OF ACTIVITIES/FUNCTIONAL AREAS

Please indicate the programmes undertaken by your NGO across different sectors during the last 5 years.

Sr. No.	*Activity*	*Name of Programme and Year*	*Target Villages / Group*	*Funding Agency / Funds in Rupees.*	*Key Achievements*
1.	Forestry (social forestry, joint forest management etc.)				
2.	Agriculture and Rural Development (training under IRDP programmes, income generating activities, village land development etc.)				
2.	Education (Primary education, non formal, adult education, Total Literacy Campaign, vocational education etc.)				
3.	Health, Family Welfare and Immunization				
4.	Women and Child Welfare				
5.	Household/cottage Industries (employment generation activities)				
6.	Animal Husbandry Activities				
7.	Any Other (Specify)				

IV. MONITORING AND SUPERVISION OF PROJECTS/ ACTIVITIES

1. Have you undertaken any monitoring and supervision activity for activities during the last five years?

   Yes/No

2. Please provide details of the monitoring and supervision mechanisms established for projects / activities undertaken during the last year.

   (i) Type of Monitoring–
   - (a) Internal monitoring
   - (b) External Monitoring
   - (c) Both internal and external monitoring

   (ii) Frequency of Monitoring–
   - (a) Bi-monthly
   - (b) Monthly
   - (c) Quarterly
   - (d) Annual
   - (e) Any other (Specify)___

V. INTERACTION AND NETWORKING

Please provide details on your interaction with the following stakeholders:

Sr. No.	*Target Segment*	*Whether Interact Yes / No*	*Frequency of Interactions*	*Quality of Interaction Satisfied / Not Satisfied*
1.	Other NGOs			
2.	Academic Institutions			
3.	Other Government departments at state/district level			
4.	Government Departments at Centre			
5.	Other independent agencies			
6.	Any other (specify)________			

VI. GENERAL INFORMATION

1. Do you get sufficient fund to support organisation's activities? Yes/No

2. Do existing policies of the government create problems in receiving fund from Government, private and other international agencies?

   - If yes, how it affects? Give three reasons

   (i)

   (ii)

   (iii)

   - Give three suggestions for improvement.

   (i)

   (ii)

   (iii)

3. Do you think that you have been able to achieve the objectives of your organisation?

   Yes/No

   - If your answer is 'No' then please state reasons for the non-achievement.

   (i)

   (ii)

   (iii)

4. Do your relationship with the other NGOs in your region is effective/very effective?

   Yes/No

   - If your answer is 'No' then please list important reasons for that.

   (i)

   (ii)

   (iii)

5. In your opinion, how the relationship could be made effective?

___

6. Do you think that NGOs have contributed for the social development in your region?

Yes/No

- If yes, mention the name of the organisation and the contribution.

	Name of the Organisation	Focus Area/s	Awards Received
(i)			
(ii)			
(iii)			

7. If you want to furnish any other information regarding the contribution of NGOs in Social Development, fundamental issues and challenges then write below.

___

___

___

SECTION-II

QUESTIONNAIRE FOR THE BENEFICIARIES OF NON-GOVERNMENTAL ORGANISATIONS (NGOs) IN VIZIANAGARAM DISTRICT ANDHRA PRADESH

Socio-Economic Profile of the Beneficiaries

1. Age

(a) 18 – 28 (b) 29 – 38 (c) 39-48 (d) 49 and above

2. Type of Family

(a) Joint (b) Nuclear

3. Caste

(a) OC (b) SC (c) ST (d) BC

4. Religion

(a) Hindu (b) Muslim (c) Christian

5. Education

(a) Illiterate (b) Primary
(c) High School (d) Intermediate

6. Income per month

(a) Below 1000 (b) 1001 – 2000
(c) 2001-3000

Beneficiary's opinion on their Development in various aspects of life:

I. Beneficiary's opinion on Development aspect;

1. What do you think about development of life?
(a) Developed (b) Partially Developed

(c) Low Developed

2. Indicate changes in the following aspects of development (in order of preference1,2,3,4)?

- Social Development ( )
- Economic Development ( )
- Political Development ( )
- Cultural & Religious Develoment ( )

II. Beneficiary's opinion on social development;

1. Is there any infrastructural development in your village?
Yes/No

2. Do you practice social evils?

   Yes/No

3. Did you find any improvement in education among the people of the village?

   (a) Improved (b) Partially Improved
   (c) Not Improved

4. What do you think on the status of women in the village?

   (a) Improved (b) Partially Improved
   (c) Not Improved

5. What is your opinion on the level of self image of the people of the village?

   (a) Improved (b) Partially Improved
   (c) Not Improved

6. What is the level of awareness on various laws related to life?

   (a) More aware/High (b)Aware/ Middle
   (c) Less aware/ Low

7. Do you know health facilities provided by the state and central governments? Yes/No

III. Beneficiaries opinion on economic development;

1. Do you have savings in the bank? Yes/No
2. Do you know how to avail bank loans? Yes/No
3. Is there any increase of assets and livestock?

   (a) Increased (b) Partially Increased

   (c) Not Increased

4. Do you think that you gained the position of self reliance?

   Yes/No

5. What do you think on experience in financial exploitation?

   (a) More/High (b) Average
   (c) Not at all

6. Do you have any improvement on level of income?

(a) Improved (b) Partially Improved
(c) Not Improved

IV. Beneficiary's opinion on political development;

1. Indicate your membership in political party?

(a) Congress (b) Telugu Desam
(c) Praja Rajyam (d) Other parties

2. What is your position as a leader?

(a) President of the Village (Surpanch)

(b) Ward Member

(c) Cooperative Society Member

(d) Leadership in SHG

(e) Other Committee Member

(f) School Committee Member

(g) No position

3. What is your level of awareness on Right to vote?

(a) More aware/ High
(b) Less aware/ Low

4. What is your level of awareness on the positions of MPs and MLAs ?

(a) More aware/ High
(b) Less aware/ Low

5. Do you have knowledge on government agencies working for development?

(a) More knowledge/ High
(b) Less Knowledge/ Low

V. Beneficiary's opinion on Religious and Cultural development;

1. Did you change from the belief on fate of life?

   (a) Changed (b) Partially Changed
   (c) Not Changed

2. Do you have faith in god ?

   (a) Strong (b) Average (c) Low

3. What is your opinion on living moral life?

   (a) Important (b) Partilly Imptortant
   (c) Unimportant

4. Do you practice cultural traits?

   (a) Rigid (b) Flexible
   (c) No practice

5. What is the level of change in belief in superstiton?

   (a) Changed (b) Partially changed
   (d) Not changed

VI. Beneficiary's opinion on efforts and functional characteristics of NGOs:

1. Do you think the efforts of NGos are important for development? Yes/No

2. Indicate the following functional characteristics as in your opinion (in order of preference 1,2,3,4,5,6,7,8)?

- Physical Appearance ( )
- Competence ( )
- Credibility ( )
- Accessibility ( )
- Responsiveness ( )
- Support and Security ( )
- Sensitivity ( )
- Communication ( )

Bibliography

Bibliography

A. Gani and Riyaz Ahmad (1995). Correlates of Quality of Work Life: An Analytical Study Indian Journal Of Industrial Relations, Volume 31, No. July 1995.

A. Hartman & J. Laird (Eds.) (1991). A Hand Book Of Child Welfare: Context, Knowledge,

A. T. Welford (1970).On the Nature of skills Penguin Books, Baltimore.

A.P.J.Abdul Kalam & Y.S. Rajan (1998). A vision for the New Millennium: Penguin Books, India.

Abha, Vijai and Prakashan (2000). Voluntary Organisations and Social Welfare, ABD Publishers, Jaipur, India.

Achla Gakhar (2002). :Kishore Balika Youjna Vol. 49, Social Welfare, Central Social Welfare Board, New Delhi, Dee. 2002 Pg. 34.

Agarwar, D. (2001). Empowerment of Rural Women in India, Social Welfare, vol.48, No.4, July, Pp. 3-4.

Alka Srivastava (2003). Voluntary Organisations In India: An Overview' Pg. 16 Social Welfare Vol. 49 Feb. 2003.

Alvi S.A. (1980)..Work values and attitudes: A review of recent research and its implications. Interchange on Educational Policy.

Amal, Mandal, (2005). Swarnajayanti Gram Swarozgar Yojana and Self Help Group : as assessment Kurukshetra, January 2005.

Anand, V. K. (2001), Avenue for Sustainable Empowerment of Rural Women Social Welfare, Vol.48, No.4, July, Pp.24-26.

Ann. A.Abbott (1999). Measuring Social Values: A Cross-Cultural Challenge For Global Practice, International Social Work: Vol. 42, No.4, October 1999.

Armando Morales and Bradford W. Sheafor (1998). Social Work: A Profession of Many Faces, 4th ed. (Boston: Allyn and Bacon, 1987).

B. P. Maithani (1995). Voluntary Organisation As Partnery, Promoting, Participatory Development Kurukshetra.

B. P. Sinha and Sarita Singh (1995). Employees Satisfaction and Its Organisational

B. T. Lawani (1999). Non-Government organisations in Development: Case Study of Solapur District). Rawat Publications, New Delhi.

B.G. Verghese (1979). Voluntary Action, A New Mission for the New Missionaries In Misra and Sundaram (eds.), Rural Area Development: Perspectives and Approaches, p. 238. New Delhi: Sterling Publishers, Private Ltd., Ballinger, (Chapter 8 and 9, pp. 115-129). Bear, Betty L., and Federico, Birnbaum-More, Philip H. Wong, Blackwell and Mortin

Basu Sisir.1994. entitled, Rural Poor; Failure of Growth Models Deccan Chronicle

Baviskar, B.S.2001. NGOs and Civil Society, Sociological Bulletin, 8 October, Vol.50,No.(1)

C. R. Kothari (1992). Research Methodology: Methods and Techniques, Wiley Eastern Limited, New Delhi.

Chambers, R. and Conway, G. R. 1992, *Sustainable Rural Livelihoods: Practical Concepts for the 21st Century,* Discussion Paper 296, Institute of Development Studies, Falmer, Sussex

Charyulu, U.V.N.1981. Voluntary Organisations and Rural Development Rural Development in India: Some Aspects, (ed.,) NIRD, Hyderabad.

Chandra Sushil (1954). Social work in Uttar Pradesh , Indian Conference of Social work

Charles Zastrow (1986). Introduction to Social welfare, Social Problems, Services and Current Issues, fourth edition Wads worth Publishing Company, California.

Chaturvedi. T.N. (Ed.), (1987). Voluntary Organisations and Development - Their Role and Functions', The Indian Journal of Public Administration, July-September, 1987, Vol. xxxiii, NO.3.

Clark,J. (1991). "Democratising Development: The Role of Voluntary Organisation", London: Earthscan.

Coutiho Noel L. (2001). Study of Quality of Health Care provided in tertiary level hospital in Mumbai, TISS Mumbai.

D Suza N.P. (1990). Relationship Between Quality of Work life an Employee commitment, TISS, Mumbai.

D. Chowdhary (1985-a). Profile of Social Welfare and Development in India, P.190.

D. Paul Chowdhary (1985-c). Profile of Social Welfare and Development in India, M.N. Publishers and Distribution in India.

D. Paul Chowdhary (1990-d). "Voluntary Effort in Social Welfare and Development ", Siddharth publishers, New Delhi.

D. Paul Chowdhary (1993-b). Handbook of Social Welfare: Fields of Social Work, Atmaram and Sons, New Delhi,3rd Edition.

Dabhi James C. (2002). The Organisational Factors Influencing tile Effectiveness of NGOs and Grassroots Organisations in Gujarat, Dept. of Sociology, School of Social Sciences, Gujarat University, Ahmedabad, 2002.

Das. S. (2003). Self Help Groups & Micro Credit – Synergic Integration, Kurukshetra, 2003

Desai, Vasant.1988. Rural Development: Experiments in Rural Development, Vol IV, Himalaya Publishing House, New Delhi.

Dhanagare, D.N.1998. NGOs and Foreign Funding, Man and Development, 20(2).

David O Renz (1998). Non-profit Organisational Effectiveness, New Delhi.

Devasia, L. (2001). Rural Women's Empowerment: A Grass Root Level Experiment. Social Welfare, Vol.48, No.4, July, Pp. 5-10.

Dr. C. S. Singhal (1998). Voluntary Action in Rural Development: OM Sons Publishers, New Delhi.

Dr. D. R. Sachdeva (2003.) Social Welfare Administration in India: Kitab Mahal Distributions, New Delhi.

Dr. Rajshree P. Mahtani (1992). Perspective in Social work, Tata Institute of Social Sciences, Mumbai.

Dwarakanath, (2003). Saving and Credit Movement in Andhra Pradesh- Participation of Rural Women, Kurukshetra, August 2003.

Eilen Gambrill and Robert Pruger (1998) : Controversial Issues In Social Work Ethics, Values And Obligations: Social Work Journal of the National Association of Social Workers, Vol. 43, NO.3 Page 286, May 1998.

Etzioni, A. (1981). "Modern Organisations", Prentice-Hall, New Delhi.

FAO. 1989. Sustainable Development and Natural Resources Management, Twenty-Fifth Conference, Paper C 89/2 - Sup. 2, Food and Agriculture Organisation, Rome.

Fisher, A. C, and Hanemann, W. 1990, Information and the Dynamics of Environmental Protection: the Concept of the Critical Period, *Scandinavian Journal of Economics* 92(3), 399-414.

Fisher, Julie. (1993). The Road from Rio: Sustainable Development and the Non-Governmental Movement in the Third World, USA: Praeger, Publisher.

Gangrade K. D. (1987). Encyclopedia of Social Work in India, Ministry of Information and Broadcasting, Govt. of India, New Delhi.

Gangrade K. D. (1971). Community Organisation, in India, Bombay, Popular Prakasham.

Garg, Pulin K. and Parikh, Indira. Crossroads of Culture-A study in the Culture of (1995) Transience, Sage, New Delhi.

Ghosh S. & Kalra S.K. (1982). Perceptional Difference in Quality of Work Life Factors Indian Journal of Tralr1lng & Development, 1982 12 (3-4) P 10-12.

Gibb C. A. (1975). Leadership , in Lindzey, G. and Aronson E., (Eds.) The Handbook of Social Psychology, Volume four, Amerind, New Delhi.

Ginger (1996). The Helping Relationship Process& Skills.

Glisson C. & Hemmelgarn A. (1998). The Effects of Organisational Climate and Inter Goel, Madan Lal and Singh V. B.

Goodman G. & Dooley D. (1976). A Framework for Help in Intended Communication. Psychotherapy Theory, Research & Practice Prentice Hall, London.

Gurumoorthy, T. R. (2000). Self Help Groups Empower Rural Women, Kurushetra, Vol.48, No.5, February, p. 36-39.

H. C. Ganguli (1999). Job Satisfaction Scales for Effective Management: Manual For Managers and Social Scientists, Concepts Publishing Co., New Delhi, Pp. 97, Indian Journal Of Industrial Relations, Vol.31, No. 1.

Hardcastle A. J. (1984). Work Values and Personality Types: A comparative study of two occupational interest groups. M.S. Thesis California State University, Long Beach.

Harshad R. Trivedi (1999). NGO: An Omnibus Myth. Paper presented at the meeting of members of Acharyakul, Gujarat Vidhyapeeth, Ahmedabad.

Haya Itzhaky (1995). Can Social Work Intervention Increase Organisational Effectiveness, International Social Work: Volume 38, NO.3 July 1995.

Herbert Aptekar (1967). The Values, Functions and Methods of Social Work in an Integrated Report of the Honolulu Seminar, If in An Inter-cultural Exploration Universals and Differences in Social Work Values, Functions, and Practice (New York: Council on Social Work Education. HRD, Hyderabad.

Hudson, Mike (1995). Managing Without Profit: The Art of Managing Third Sector Organisations, Penguin, England.

Jackie Powell (2002). Changing Conditions of Social Work Research, British Journal Of Social Work 2002.

Jeanne C. Marsh (2003). To Thine Own Ethics Code Be True: Social Work Vol.48 NO.1 Jan 2003.

Jimmy Dabhi, (2005) NGOs' Response to Violence against the Marginalised and Discriminated Communities, Social Action-January-March 2005, Volume 55.

June Hopps & Elaine (1980). Profession of Social Work Contemporary Characteristics A Critique of the Working Definition Social Work Journal of National Association of Social Worker.

Kadushin and Regina Kulys, (1996). Job Satisfaction Among Social Work Discharge

Karivelil Sureshbabu (2001). Patients Satisfaction: A Comparative Study Between a Public and Private Hospital, Mumbai, TISS, Mumbai.

Kher B. G. (1950). Training for Social Work, An Introductory Survey, New Delhi.

Koeske and Koeske (1989). Construct Validity of the Maslach Burnout Inventory: A Critical Review and Reconceptualisation. Journal of Applied Behavioral Science, 25 (25),131-144.

Korten, F. and Siy, R.F. (1988). Transforming a Bureaucracy, West Hartford, Conn.: Kumarian Press.

Kulshrestha, L. R. et. al. (2002). NGO in Micro Finance Partners in Rural Development Kuruksheta, February issues.

Kurukshetra, L. R. (2004). Rajiv Gandhi National Drinking Water Mission Committed to providing Safe Drinking Water.

Kabra, Kamal Nayan. (1985). Confused or Camouflaged, Yojna Issue on Testing Voluntary Agencies, June 16-30, pp. 9-11.

Kapoor, A.K., Dharm Vir Singh. (1997). Rural Development Through NGOs, Rawat Publications, Jaipur.

Kapoor, Rakesh (1996). Voluntary Action Survival, Politics and Transformation, Social Action, Vol. 46, January-March.

Little, I.M.D. and Mirrlees, J. A. 1974, *Project Appraisal and Planning for Less Developed Countries,* Heinemann, London.

Louise C Johnson (1989). Social Work Practice : A Generalist Approach, 6th edition Boston, Allyn and Bacon.

Ludwig, D., Hilborn, R. and Walters, C. (1993) Uncertainty, Resource Exploitation, and Conservation: Lessons from History, *Science* 260, 17, 36.

Lakshmaiah,T. (1999). Tribal Development: Role of Voluntary Organisations, Kurukshetra.

Lucy, T.V. (1993). Social Reforms to Voluntarism in India, Legal News and Views, December pt., No.3: p. 400.

M. A. Muttalib (1987). Voluntarism and Development-Theoretical Perspectives. Indian Journal of Public Administration, Vol. XXXIII (July-Sep.).

M.K. Shome.G.Bhardwaj and A. Titus (1996). Time Management in relation to Work Values across Managerial Levels in a Public Sector Organisation, Indian Journal of Industrial Relations, Vol. 2. M. L. Dantwa, Harsh Sethi.

M. S. Gore (1985). Social Aspect of Development, Jaipur, Raval Publisher.

Macmillan and Max Siporin, (1975). Introduction to Social Work Practice, New York.

Mahakal Sandhaya Mahesh (1995). Perception of Patients Satisfaction, TISS, Mumbai.

Mane Alka Mahendra (1996). Study of Job Satisfaction on Nursing Staff in Municipal General Hospital, Mumbai TISS. Mark Robinson, John Farrington.

Markandya, A. and Pearce, D. W. (1991). Development: The Environment and the Social Rate of Discount, *World Bank Research Observer* 6(2), 137-52.

Md. Mosharraf Hossain and Md. Tariqul Islam (1999). Quality of Working Life and Job satisfaction of Government Hospital Nurses in Bangladesh: Source IJIR, Vol.3, January. p. 293.

Meher C. Nanavatty and Mehta Madhavi (2002). A Study of Professional Values, Value Conflict and Coping Mechanisms of HRD Professionals in India (Ph.D.) XLRI, Jamshedpur.

Michael, Woolcock, (1998). Social Capital and Development: Toward a Theoretical Synthesis and Policy Framework (Theory and Society).

Michal Banton (1968). Anthropological, Voluntary Association, in David L Sills (ed), International Encyclopaedia of Social Sciences, Vol. 16, New York, The Macmillan Co. and the Free Press, 1968, p.358.

Milton Rokeach (1973). The Nature of Human Values.

Mishra, A. K. (2004). Social Capital-Alternative Model for Viable Development. Kurukshetra.

Mladen Knezevic. Social Work Students and Work Values: International Social Work, Vol. 42-44, October 1999, p. 420-428.

Muriel W. Pumphrey (1959). The Teaching of Values and Ethics in Social Work Education Vol. 13 of the Curriculum Study Council on Social Work Education, New York.

Mehta, P.C. (1994). Voluntary Organisation and Tribal Development

Nityananda, (2000). The Emerging Role of NGOs in Rural Development of India, Vol. 30, Nos. 344, (Sep-Dec).

N.R. Inamdar (1987). Role of Voluntarism in Development. Indian Journal of Public Administration. Vol. XXXIII (July-September 1987), No.3: 420.

Nair B. (1995). HRD Facilitators Programme for NGOs. Renewal, No. 1, September.

Narasimhan, S. (1999). Empowering Women: An Alternative Strategies from Rural India, New Delhi, Sage Publications.

Noorjahan Bawa (1997). NGOs in Development, Theory & Practice, Kanishka Publishers, New Delhi.

P.D. Kulkarni (1983). Voluntary Action, The Myth and Reality, p. 6. John Barnabas Memorial Lecture (1982), New Delhi: NIPCCD.

P.D. Kulkarni (1998). NGOs in the Changing Scenario, Uppal Publishing House, New Delhi.

Parikh K. S. (1999). India Development Report 1999-2000 Mumbai: Indira Gandhi Institute of Development Research.

Parmar M.N. (2003). Study of Organisational Effectiveness with Reference to Job Satisfaction, Employees Effectiveness and Personality Traits, (Ph.D.) Faculty of Social Work, M. S. University of Baroda, 2003.

Patel Chhaya (2000). Assessing Social Components of Integrated Child Development Services in Tribal Regions of Gujarat (Ph.D.) Faculty of Social Work, M. S. University, Baroda.

Paul Davidson Reynolds, (1975). A Primer in Theory Construction (Indianapolis, In Books Merrill,)

Phillips Anjali (1997). A Study of Functionaries in Human Care Agencies in Indore, (M. P.). Faculty of Social work, M. S. University of Baroda.

Pincus, Allen and Minahan (1975). Social Work Practice : Model and Method, Itasca; F, E. Itasca; F. E. Peacock Publishers Inc.

Prakash Karat (1988). Foreign Funding and the Philosophy of Voluntary Organisations, New Delhi: National Book Centre.

Prasad, (2003). Social Interaction: Concept, Meaning and Approach (Part-1), Kurukshetra, Vol.51 No.8 June 2003.

Pravin Visaria (1998). Social Change Through Voluntary Action Edited by Sage Publications, New Delhi.

PRIA (1991). Voluntary Organisation in India: A Study of History. Roles and Future Challenges.

Pruthi, R.K. (2000). Manual of NGOs How to Manage, Crest Publishing House, New Delhi.

Raj Kumar Siwach (2003). Prospective Role of VO's: in Tenth Plan, p. No. 1.3 Social Welfare, Vol. 49.

Rajni Kothari (1987). Voluntary Organisation in a Plural Society. *IJPA*. Vol. XXXIII (July-Sept), No. 3:437. Encyclopedia Brittanica (Micro Paedia, Ready Reference and Index) Vol. X, 1997, p. 491.

Rajni Kothari (1997 July-Sept.). Voluntary Organisation in a Plural Society, Indian Journal of Public Administration, Vol. XXXIII Pg. 433.

Rama J. Joshi and Baldev R. Sharma (1999). Determinants Of Managerial Job Satisfaction in a Private Organisation *IJIR* Vol. 33 No. 1.

Ramchandran K. (1990). Job satisfaction, Job Involvement and Organisational Commitment of Police Station Staff in Mumbai City TISS, Mumbai.

Ramchandran V. (1995). Social Oraganisations in the Era of Globalisation. Seminar, Vol. 447.

Rao, R. (2005). Women's Groups Herald: A Wind Change in Rural Uttaranchal, *Kurukshetra*, January 2005.

Rao, R. et. al, (2005). Gangadevipally Village- All Round Participation in Village Administration, Kurukshetra, January 2005.

Rao, V. D. and Rao, A. P. (2000), Swasakti Bank of the Community, By the Community, For the Community, *Social Welfare*, August, pp.3-8.

Rao, V. D. (2000), Emerging Leadership of Women in Institutions of Local Governance: A Study in Andhra Pradesh, *Social Action*, Vol. 53 April-June.

Rino J. Patti (2000). The Hand book of Social Welfare Management: Sage Publications, Inc.

Robert D. Herman and Robertson, (1981). Voluntary Social Services, Oxford.

Robinson, M. A. (1991). Evaluating the Impact of NGOs in Rural Poverty Alleviation-India Country Study, Working Paper no. 49, London: ODI.

Ronald C (1978). Educating the Baccalaureate Social Worker. Cambridge, MA.

Rubin, Allen and Babbie (1989). Research Method for Social Work, California: Wadsworth Publishing Co.

Raj Kumar.(2002). Capacity Building of Panchayats for Rural Development: Some Emerging Areas for NGOs.

Satyanarayana,G. (1992). Changing Agrarian Structure and Labour Relations, Rawat Publications, Jaipur.

Satyanarayana, G.(1998). Voluntary Organisation and Emancipation of Dalit Women, In Y.B. Abasayulu (ed.,), Women in Developing Society.

Sharma, B.D. (1984). Planning for Tribal Development, Prachi Prakashan, New Delhi.

Singh, D.N. (1985). Introduction: A Prologue to Rural Development Strategies in India.

Singh, Madhuri and Singh, K.N. (1985). Voluntary Agencies: Their Role in Rural Development in India. In K.N. Singh and D.N.Singh (eds.) Rural Development in India, Varanasi.

Singh.L Foundation, Sahay, B. K. (2002). Empowering Community for Sustainable Livelihood through Jankar System, Kuruksheta, February issues.

Savant Gokuldas Vasant (1996). Job Satisfaction in Paramedical Workers TISS, Mumbai.

Sudha, K. and Bhargava, B.S. (2000). Panchayats and NGOs in Social Change, Kurukshetra, Vol. 48, No. 10.

Shivani Dharmaraja (2001). NGOs as Prime Movers Sectoral Action for Social Development, Kanishka Publishers, New Delhi-110 002.

Sinha, K. (ed) (2000). Empowerment of Women in South Asia, AMDISA and SAARC. Hyderabad.

Sivasubramanian, M. N. (1999). Credit Based Poverty Alleviation Programme: Innovative Approach, Kurushetra, Vol. 48, No. 2, November, pp. 37-41.

Smith and Freedman (1972). Voluntary Associations; Perspective in the Literature, Cambridge (Mass) Hardward University Press.

Snehlata Chandra (2001). Non-Governmental Organisations: Structure, Relevance, and Function, Kanishka Publishers, New Delhi-110 002.

Sonke Schmidt (1995). International Social Work: Social Security in Developing Countries: Basic Tenets and Fields of State Intervention Vol. 38, No. 1, Jan. 1995.

S. Satish (eds.), (1993). Non-Governmental Organisation and the State in Asia, p. 93 London, New York: Routledge.

Stephen T. Moore and Michael J. Kelly (1996). Quality Now: Moving Human Services and S. Satish (eds.), (1993). Non-Governmental Organisation and the State in Asia, p. 93 London, New York: Routledge. Organisation Toward A Consumer Orientation,

Srivastava, S.P.(1999). Nature of Voluntary Action in India Today: A Critique, *Social Action*, Vol.49, January-March.

Sudan Mohan Singh (2001). Study of Job Satisfaction Amongst Grassroots Level Workers in Parmandal Block of District Jammu TISs, Mumbai.

Sujit Bunker Roy (1987). Voluntary Agencies in Development. Voluntary Agencies in Development. IJPA (July-September), p. 547.

Sundari S. and Geeta, N. (2000). Poverty, Credit and Micro Enterprises: A Gender Study, Kurushetra, Vol. 49, No. 2, November, pp. 26-35.

Sundram, 1.S. (1986). Voluntary Agencies and Rural Development B. R. Publishing Corporation, Delhi.

Syed Noman Ahmad (1997). Rapid Rural Transformations Through Voluntary Action, M.D. Publications Pvt. Ltd., New Delhi.

Srivastava, S.P.(1999). Nature of Voluntary Action in India Today: A Critique, *Social Action*, Vol. 49, January-March.

Tandon R. (1989). NGO-Government Relations: A Source of Life or A Kiss of Death, New Delhi: Society for Participatory Research in Asia.

Tandon R. (2002). Civil Society and Decentralisation. (An Interview Presentation). Participation and Governance. Vol. 8, (23).

Tata Institute of Social Sciences, Mumbai (2002). Compendium on Management of Non-Profit Organisations in the Changing Development Scenario by Department of Social Welfare Administration in Coordination with Social Work Education and Practice Cell, Tata Institute of Social Sciences, Mumbai.

Taylor M.S.Covaleski, M.A.(1982). Predicting Individual's Turnover and Internal Transfer Behaviour. Paper Presented at an Annual Meeting of the Midwestern Psychological Association, Minneapolis, May 6-8.

Thomas J. Cartin (2000). Principles and Practices of Organisational Performance Excellence By, Prentice - Hall of India Pvt. Ltd., New Delhi.

Thomas L. (1994). HRD Needs of Non-governmental Organisations, Occasional Paper-2. Ahmedabad: Academy of Human Resource Development.

Timothy J.Flanagan,W.Wesley Johnson, Katherine Bennett (1996). Job Satisfaction Among Correctional Executives: A Contemporary Portrait of Wardens of State Prisons for Adults: The Prison Journal, Vol. 76, No. 4, December 1996, 385-397, Sage Publications Inc.

Tudu Sheila J. (1982). Social Intervention Role of Workers in Social Welfare Agencies "Study of Institutional Care Agencies under Social Defense in Baroda City" (Ph.D) Faculty of Social Work, The M.S.University of Baroda.

U.Y.N.Charyulu, and V.K. Natrajan, (1980). Voluntary Organisation and Rural Development, Rural Development Digest, (April), P. 106, Nird, Hyderabad.

V. N. Raghu (2001). Services Marketing, Himalaya Publishing House, New Delhi.

V.G. Nandekar (1987). Voluntary Association: A Strategy in Development. *IJPA* (July-Sept), pp. 465-81.

Varshney K.G. (2004). Management: Productivity Digest, May-June 2004.

Vijaya Kumar, S. (2002). Devadasis – Social Problems in India – Series 1, National Commission for Women, Hyderabad: Council for Social Development (memio).

Werner W. Boeham (1958). The Nature of Social Work.

William Beveridge (1979). Voluntary Action in a Challenging World, London, Bedford Square Press, National Council of Social Services, 1979.

William E. Gorden 1964. Building Social Work knowledge: National Association of Social Work, New York.

Yardi Meeta, Mona Amin, Darshita Acharya (2000). A Study of Women Social Work Professionals in Different Fields (MSW) Faculty of Social Work, M. S. University of Baroda.

Yoshitomi, Masaru, (2001). Quoted in Social Safety Nets Seminar: Executive Summary of Proceedings (http://www.adbi.org/PDF/social%20safety%20nets.pdf, 9 March 2002).

Zoya Taylor A (1999). Values, Theories and Methods in Social Work Education: Culturally Transferable Core, International Social Work: Volume 42, No. 3.

Index

T

U

V

W

Z